Good Que.

Good Question!

The Art of Asking Questions
To Bring About Positive Change

Judy Barber

First Published In Great Britain 2005
by www.BookShaker.com

Typeset in Georgia

Cover Art by Amelia Barber
Photos of Judy Barber by Irving Bastin

To my daughter and her generation, who are pearls beyond price

CONTENTS

PART EIGHT: ALLOWING FOR, FINDING AND CREATING QUESTIONS

ACKNOWLEDGEMENTS

I could fill a book with the names of people who have inspired me – and in fact I just have! Many thanks indeed to my delightful contributors and publishers.

I also acknowledge my gratitude to and affection for my wonderful family and friends, along with my teachers, mentors, facilitators, lecturers, students, coaches, clients and colleagues past and present, and in fact all who have lent me a hand along the way to here.

And then there's my gratitude to the writers of so very many books and magazines I've read. Their thought, creativity and effort have enriched my life.

And to you, the reader, my appreciation of whatever you contribute to the lives of others and to making the world a better place.

FOREWORD

BY COEN DE GROOT
INTERNET STRATEGY COACH, OWNER "EURO COACH LIST"
www.EuroCoachList.com / www.MentorCoaches.com / www.CoachCoen.com

What makes a good question?

What is the ultimate coaching question?

What is the best question you have ever been asked?

What is the best question you have ever asked?

And the bonus question: How many questions are there in this foreword?

When I was reading this book I was reminded of the power of questions and struck by the wealth of experience and insight of the authors. Judy has asked the right questions to encourage an impressive group of individuals to contribute their words and wisdom. The questions the contributors ask are making a real difference to many people's lives.

As a professional coach and owner of Europe's premier coaching community (www.eurocoachlist.com) my life is also full of questions and here are some questions to ask yourself whilst reading this book: What are the thoughts and the assumptions behind the question? Why did the author ask this question, and why did they phrase it this way? What makes the author successful? What are the key elements of the author's views or system? What else can I learn from the author and from this story? How can I use this? How will I make the question my own? What words would I use?

In some of the chapters the authors have kindly spelled out many of the answers. In some cases you will have to work at it.

And here is a final question: With questions being so powerful, and there being so many to choose from, how do you know which one to ask?

Keep asking the questions, question the answers and question the questions. And above all, enjoy the journey and enjoy this great book.

PREFACE

BY RICHARD WILKINS
INTERNATIONAL BEST SELLING AUTHOR
AND INSPIRATIONAL SPEAKER
www.theministryofinspiration.com

The wonderful thing about a question is that it needs to be answered, and *Good Question!* asks some of the most amazing questions imaginable. The other amazing thing about *Good Question!* is that you are getting so many people's opinions. I've worked with many of the people who have contributed to Judy Barber's Book and I know just how Amazing they are and the results they are achieving. So they must be asking the right questions!

In my career as a professional speaker I always notice a huge difference in the audience when I ask a question. The whole energy of the room changes. My belief is that most people most of the time are looking in the wrong filing cabinet. They are looking for external answers to internal problems. The beauty of questions is that they get people to look in the right filing cabinet!

At a core level we all know that the only reason we are not getting the right answers is because we're not asking the right questions. This is the reason I love asking people questions and this is the power of a *Good Question!*

I woke up in the year 1990. What I discovered was so amazing that I had no choice but to share the wisdom I found. In this book you are blessed to discover the insights of some truly wise people who, like me, have woken up, stopped blaming, taken responsibility and begun creating the lives they deserve. I love the team effort that has gone into *Good Question!* In this book you are blessed to hear the wisdom of the 'virtual tribe' that Judy has gathered and led.

As a reader, you would be hard pushed to find elsewhere so much diverse wisdom in a single publication. You don't need to read from cover to cover and can search through and find the relevant sections. This offers a unique style as well as amazing content. Try it now if you wish. Stop reading this preface, browse through and you will soon find a section that will guide and help you. Hopefully you will remember to return to finish the preface! However, with such amazing content do not be surprised by how enticing you find the pages. With laser point accuracy you can home in on the specific challenges affecting your life now and resolve them.

The beauty of *Good Question!* is that by asking the right questions it creates the right 'search engines' within us, but, much more than this, each section then gently guides us with wisdom and insight that Merlin himself would be proud of. One only needs to look to the most popular movies and it is clear that more than anything else, people want magic in their lives. As you read through the pages you will find many wonderful spells you can use to create the magic that you want and deserve.

Until recently the missing ingredient eluded me. Now I know why so many people do not have what they want. The reason is they do not believe deep down that they deserve what they want. This book will help you deserve what you want. It will help you value yourself more and increase your self-esteem.

Applying these simple yet profound messages can and will open up a new world to you. *Good Question!* is a small key that can open a big door.

Good Question! is perfectly timed. It arrives with us at a time when human consciousness is set to go broadband as values change and people re-assess their lives and place more value on the time they spend on this planet. In that sense the wisdom contained within these pages is invaluable, priceless. Enjoy your newfound friend, this book, and make it a companion you travel with, regardless of which direction you may choose to take.

Remember, real change is when we see the same old things differently.

INTRODUCTION

Welcome to *Good Question!*, an anthology of good questions to give you more ways to think about things and to open up and develop constructive conversations. It is a book that grew from a question I found myself asking about how communication can improve situations on a massive scale. It developed into something like this:

'How can people use questions to create positive change in the world?'

It's an interesting question because asking and giving can appear as opposites, yet in this sense they are not. The right question can be a miraculous gift. When we ask questions amazing breakthroughs can happen, both locally and globally.

As I asked people this question they responded with such enthusiasm that I knew I was onto something. None of the contributors featured in this book took much persuading! People, quite naturally, want to make a positive difference in life.

Many people have visions of how wonderful life can become on our earth, while others have given up on vision, or never knew it was theirs to have. Many of us struggle with day-to-day realities and having a vision can seem like a kind of ephemeral luxury. We may not have time for day dreaming, and on a global scale perhaps we don't have any spare time at all, but vision is our life-raft and can help us to carry on, one task at a time, in the face of the magnitude of all that humanity faces.

Visionary answers to all the problems we face will stem from the questions we ask ourselves.

Along with my own writing I have assembled chapters from 27 contributors about the questions they use to get results. These people are coaches, writers, facilitators, speakers and leaders. I cherry-picked them as people who are very actively involved one way or another with helping people to make changes, and as people with fascinating things to say.

Some of the material here is slanted towards self-development-questions to ask yourself, some towards one-to-one conversations such as coaching conversations and some towards working with groups, but there's a general undertow of working both on one's own development <u>and</u> contributing to life. So this book is for you if you want to find inspiration for inhabiting your own life in new ways <u>and</u> if you, like just about everyone I speak to, know that your life is for more than just yourself. Perhaps you want to take on making more effective contributions to the lives of others and/or to life on a bigger scale through your business, work or voluntary activities. This might be family relationships, disaster relief, developing a positive culture or vision in a business, improving the environment, politics, the arts, the public sector, the media, community work or charity. Whatever it is, at the core change will be initiated in meetings between people at which results get analysed, problems discussed, visions get dreamed up, goals identified and steps plotted. In those conversations good questions are invaluable for thorough, imaginative and practical thinking. Good questions give you more choices.

Who is it for?

Good Questions! is a book for coaches, counsellors, trainers, teachers and the like, who specifically use forms of helpful conversation in work and want to find new possibilities and ways to work.

It is also just as much a book for you as parents, leaders, friends, team members, entrepreneurs, partners, managers, writers, carers, directors, family members and in fact for you in any role in which you want to have effective conversations and through them to make effective contributions to life on any scale.

Questions are the stock-in-trade of Life and Business Coaches and others who use a 'coach approach' in their work – which rapidly increasing numbers of people are doing. For you this book is a treasure chest. Be surprised, lift the lid. Rummage and lift strings of gems into the light. Many of the contributors coach, and you can find out exactly what kinds of questions and processes we use.

It's also for you if you want to know more about coaching and how different people coach. Is coaching happening in your workplace or have you noticed it in the media? Find out more. Are you interested in becoming a coach? Are you thinking of hiring a coach? Reflect on what might be possible with coaching.

How to use this book

The Table of contents is a menu of good questions in itself, so you can use that as a starting point and read up on questions that intrigue you.

I've grouped the questions under headings, so that you can explore questions on a topic that is relevant to you at the moment.

You could dip in at random or start with contributors whose work already interests you.

Or you could read it from start to finish as an exploration of the power and variety of questions and for an overview of the kinds of thinking going on in coaching and related interesting fields.

Once you have found your way around *Good Question!* please keep coming back to it as a reference book. Glancing back through the menu of questions and studying up on a particular question or series of questions can prepare you for specific situations and increase your options in working creatively with what life brings towards you.

And, which might be most important of all, you can be inspired by *Good Question!* to develop new questions of your own.

Judy Barber
www. judybarber.net

Judy Barber

PART ONE: MOVING FORWARD

I'm beginning this book with three very different chapters that have something to say about going forward. Mine is about cultivating and allowing optimism. Mark Forster's is about planning and organising so that projects will go smoothly from the start. David Ure's is about freeing oneself from outdated ways of thinking so that it is indeed possible to move forward positively.

What might you achieve with optimism, organisation and freedom from past negative thinking?

Judy Barber

HOW GOOD CAN YOU STAND IT?

BY JUDY BARBER

I first remember seeing this question written in the dirt on the back of a van, long before I knew anything about Life or Business Coaching. I like it because it is witty and at the same time points to the very common inclination people have towards stopping themselves from allowing their life to get better and better. It's an unexpected question, and this unexpectedness points to the possibility that coaching questions in general have for allowing new thought.

The Antidote To Murphy's Law

'Murphy's Law' states that things will go wrong in any given situation. It is most commonly formulated as "if anything can go wrong, it will." and too often we find ourselves believing it to be true. Murphy's Law has become something of an institution with many pessimistic, though often humorous, "truisms" branching off from it. As you take a look at just a few of the examples below you'll see how asking, "How good can you stand it?" provides an optimistic counter-balance.

MURPHY'S LAWS

Nothing is as easy as it looks.

Everything takes longer than you think.

Anything that can go wrong will go wrong.

If anything simply cannot go wrong, it will anyway.

If you perceive that there are four possible ways in which a procedure can go wrong, and circumvent these, then a fifth way, unprepared for, will promptly develop.

Left to themselves, things tend to go from bad to worse.

If everything seems to be going well, you have
obviously overlooked something.

Nature always sides with the hidden flaw.

Whenever you set out to do something, something
else must be done first.

Every solution breeds new problems.

Just looking at this list of "laws" it becomes obvious that humans are very creative when it comes to focusing on the negative. And while the laws are funny and accurate at times they are also very dangerous if given too much relevance in our lives. We often live with negativity all around us; depression, anger, low self-esteem, frustration, lack of direction to name just some. So how can we shake off this negativity that may be generations old? How can we catch ourselves when we go into a pessimistic tailspin? How can we lift ourselves up again after we hit the ground with a same-old Murphy's Law thud?

What If Murphy's Law Is Self-Imposed?

"How good can you stand it?" points to a different possibility. It suggests that much of the negativity around us might be self-imposed. We even translate positive experiences into negative ones by wearing negativity goggles...

My partner is being nice → what's he/she after?

Business is going well → it's too good to last.

He/she likes me → but a good-looking person like that wouldn't really be interested in me.

I know they said I should apply → but they'll probably give the job to someone younger.

If you've grown up expecting things to be difficult, or if you've taken on someone else's critical view of you, then how can you imagine that things might, reliably, go well? What if you have built a personal identity of someone habitually unlucky or flawed? What if your identity is now what people have come to expect?

The biggest self-development step of all might simply to be cheerful and optimistic in life, regardless of what is happening, rather than bowing to your negative conditioning.

I went to see the Dalai Lama once and so many people were there that some of us had to be in another auditorium with a large video screen. The Dalai Lama made a point of coming through to our auditorium at the end of the talk to see us. He said, "Be a happy person." That really is all I can remember of the entire talk, a small figure telling us to be happy. The Tibetan religious leader is hardly a naive person and is of course alive to the sufferings of so many people in the world. So what did he mean? My interpretation was that we should take on being happy as an activity, a conscious choice of state, rather than reacting, as if powerless, to what happens to us and around us.

Taking Control

There's a part of me that can't believe I'm writing this. Where's emotional integrity if you go round being happy even if you are not? Positive Thinking? Dangerous new age piffle? Personally, I'm not interested in emotional dishonesty or "papering over the cracks", but I did take on what the Dalai Lama said. He's from a Buddhist lineage which encourages the discipline of awareness. I assume his "being happy" to be a product of that. If one is aware of the nuances of one's emotional state there's the possibility of taking control, of noticing a depression or an anger before it has a chance to take hold and take over.

I'm not suggesting one should never grieve, cry or otherwise express difficult emotions, but I am pointing to the distinction between expressing natural emotion and choosing to react negatively to things that happen in life.

So, next time all is going well and you encounter a problem of some kind then simply acknowledge it, deal with it and make an active choice to feel about it however you wish.

Difficult Moments

Imagine the scene. You've been in a relationship with someone for a while when one day their ex-partner rings up out of the blue. During the moments that follow your partner becomes preoccupied and distant.

Now if you were to "let a gremlin in" you might start saying things like "It was too good to last", "They always go back to their ex", "Nobody would want to stay with me once they really know what I'm like".

At a time like that, when it seems as if a new relationship is floundering, the Dalai Lama would have us be a happy person? Yes. Happy people get on and do things. Happy people look for the good in the situation, find a cheering word to say or look beyond themselves to what they can do for others. At the very least they put good music on and clean the house or go outside for a breath of fresh air.

When you're busy being a happy person you don't spread negativity. You don't say "What did he/she want this time then?" or "Who does he/she think he/she is ringing you when she knows you are with me?"

Glitches happen. Things can go wrong. Situations can change and external factors can get in the way of us having what we wanted. "How good can you stand it?" can be asked at the moment when the glitch happens, to remind us that there is an alternative to recognising the glitch, claiming it as our own and hanging on to it as we plummet, casually saying "I knew something like this would happen."

"How good can you stand it?" opens the door to the possibility of making a conscious choice to deal with things in a different way, free of past conditioning. It gives us the opportunity to imagine that things can work out better than we led ourselves to believe in the past. It's about being open to more happiness, success, love, money or whatever we want.

How Can You Make Sure You Don't Self-Sabotage?

Okay, so after reading this you feel inspired to react differently. So how do you make sure you apply this lesson when faced with the real world? I've had experiences of going on a workshop, reading an inspiring book or having a special conversation and resolving to act in a way that is free from past patterns, only to find that resolution hard to keep alive when I went back into my "normal" life. To be honest, there have been times when the resolve has vanished quite quickly. That's when "How good can you stand it?" might be a good question to remember, as shorthand for:

- "Whoops! Watch out for self-sabotage!"

- "I don't have to be affected by their limited view of what is possible for me."

- "Can I figure out a way for this to work out better than it looks as if it can right now?"

- "Can I allow myself this good fortune without messing things up by behaving like a four year old having a tantrum?"

- "What would the Dalai Lama do now?"

- or whatever else needs to be asked at that particular moment to keep perspective and stay happy.

When *you* change, others who are used to you having a certain identity, might find it hard to deal with; so they may react (unwittingly or not) to reinforce your old identity and past habits. Your optimism might carry them along or open up new possibilities for them and if so, great. If not, what can you do to support yourself in creating a better future for yourself and others? The "How good can you stand it?" question might be a reminder to get support before you lose sight of what you are seeing as possible. Working with a coach provides this kind of support in spades, as do supportive friends and continuous learning.

Once, when I was struggling to stay on top of various things, I had gone for a rare day out while a friend looked after my little daughter. I came home to find the friend had written quite extravagant positive affirmations about me on coloured paper and stuck them up all round my house. It was heart warming and funny and was the best possible medicine because it put me in touch with my positive attributes again. It was a reminder that, yes, I can stand it very good indeed!

How Good Can We Stand It?

One more thing I want to suggest about 'How good can you stand it?' is to relate the question to visions and goals. Relate it to personal visions for yourself, for others and for the world as a whole. It would be hard not to have heard or read the question "Who are you to play small?" Its message is that to limit ourselves and hide behind excuses is arrogant and selfish; we have to go for it in every area of life. So

'How good can you stand it?' is a reminder that we all have to get past limiting beliefs and make our fullest individual contributions to life.

Learnings And Actions From This Chapter

- Unexpected questions can literally make you think.
- Resist "Murphy's Law" thinking.
- Consider whether you have control of being cheerful.
- Watch out for self-sabotage.
- Get support for resisting other people's negativity.
- Find ways to remind yourself of how good you *can* stand it.
- We all have to get past limiting beliefs to make our full contribution to life.

Finally, if you haven't washed your car for a while, what about writing "How good can you stand it?" in the dust on the back? It might just change someone's life...

WHAT NEEDS TO BE DONE NOW?

BY MARK FORSTER

Photo by Kaia Means

Have you ever been in the situation where you have a major project that you want to carry out, but can never quite find the time to get moving on it? Or perhaps you have started out with great enthusiasm on some new idea but after a few weeks or months it has petered out because it has got swamped by all the other calls on your time?

Very often the projects we are putting off are essential to the future success of our work or business. As a coach I get accustomed to hearing potential clients saying things like: "I really need to do some more marketing, but I just don't have the time." This can be translated as, "I don't have time to do the really important things because of all the less important things I have to do."

When she came to me for coaching, Adriana had spent several years building up her successful design business and had become so busy filling orders that she no longer had time to spend looking for more clients. Unfortunately about 80% of her work came from two major clients and one of them had given notice. She was becoming increasingly worried about what would happen if the other one ceased to use her as well. Her worrying wasn't doing any good, and she was becoming aware that she really must do something about the situation – if only so she could sleep at night.

These are very common experiences. We frequently know exactly what we want to do and what we need to do in order to achieve it, but somehow find it very difficult to make the connection between the idea in our minds and the reality of actually taking day-by-day action to get it done.

A lot of this difficulty we have in introducing new projects is due to the fact that we fail to ask ourselves the question, "What needs to be done now?" This is one of my favourite coaching questions because it ties theoretical discussion down to real-world actions that actually need to be carried out within the next few days. One of the most important things that needs "to be done now" at the start of any project is the construction of a framework which will keep the project moving.

I don't of course just limit the use of "What needs to be done now?" to coaching. It is one I apply to my own work at the start of a new project or a new phase of an existing project. It is particularly important when the project is one that cannot be started on immediately.

Something that any coach has to do frequently with clients is to give them a framework for carrying out projects. Whatever the nature of the project, there are always three stages to preparing for it. These are:

1. Designing the desired future reality

2. Appraising the present reality

3. Establishing the path between the present reality and the future reality

This three-part process applies whether the project is large or small, complicated or simple. It applies whether we are talking about building an irrigation system for an African farm or organising a lift rota for taking children to school.

Adriana identified that she needed to have a better mix of clients, so that instead of trying to replace the big client with another big client she would seek to fill the gap with a mixture of medium and small clients. That would give her much more flexibility. So she drew up an ideal specification of the number and size of clients she was looking for.

In the first stage the coach will work with the client to construct a clear and compelling vision of where they want to be. In the second stage the coach encourages them to carry out a realistic appraisal of exactly where they are now in relation to the vision. In the third stage, they answer the question, "How do I get from here to there?" Even better, they can imagine themselves inhabiting their future reality and ask, "How did I get here from there?"

At this point the client has a vision and has a plan. But it's precisely at this point that things often get stuck. This is the moment at which the planning has to be translated into action.

The problem is that the client is not initiating the project on a blank canvas. If we were the client then we would know this only too well. We probably already have more work than we know what to do with. The new project has somehow to be fitted in among all the conflicting priorities we already have.

The fact is that most people do not have any effective system in their lives for taking on new work. The result is that they can construct visions and plan as much as they like, but their project will always founder because it is yet another piece of work being added to all the work which is already not getting done properly.

So after going through the three-stage process outlined above, the discussion must always be grounded in reality by asking the question "What needs to be done now?"

The answer to the question must always include the construction of a framework by which the new project is introduced, given space and protected.

Let's see how this might apply in respect to a project such as writing a chapter for a book. This is a relatively simple project, but nevertheless it is one which many people would have trouble with. The reason they would have trouble is because they don't establish when accepting the project how and when they are going to do the work.

In theory it's all very easy. All the editor of a book like this one has to do is agree the details of the chapters with the contributors, give them a deadline to work to and wait for the chapters to arrive. On the deadline all the chapters will be ready for final editing and compilation.

That's the theory. But of course anyone who has ever tried to edit a book knows how extremely difficult it is to prise chapters out of contributors. And that is not surprising if you look at how most contributors go about the process of integrating the writing project into their existing workload.

Well actually that's the problem. They don't go through any process of integrating the project into their existing workload. They will get the writing done when the pain of not doing it becomes greater than the pain of doing it. And that may well be after weeks of chasing by the editor. And it will usually be at the expense of some of their other work, so a chain reaction of further lateness is started throughout all their projects.

A similar pattern applies to all their work. They plan projects but never really answer the question of when and how they are going to do all the work involved.

The question "What needs to be done now?" is crucial to the process of integrating the new project. Let's apply that to the chapter writing example, specifically the writing of this chapter for this book. Can I do a little better than the average book contributor whose portrait I have just sketched?

Let's see. Today is 19 November and the deadline for the chapter is 6 December. As I write these words I am on the final draft of the chapter. It should be finished by tomorrow at the latest. It hasn't got in the way of any other work because I made sure that it was properly introduced into my workload. Let's see how that happened and look at the sort of mental process I went through in order to plan the project.

A few weeks ago, when I made the decision to contribute this chapter I could have expressed my decision like this:

"I will write a 2,000 word chapter for Judy Barber's book."

Now no decision means anything unless it is tied down to a deadline, so the next stage was to agree a date by which I would have delivered the chapter to Judy. My decision could now be expressed as:

"I will write a 2,000 word chapter for Judy Barber's book by 6th December."

Most people get as far as this during their planning process. But they then founder when it comes to putting the decision into action. It's easy to see why this happens. When I made this commitment 6th December was over a month away. It couldn't be started immediately because of other commitments. Now normally what tends to happen here is that the project is put on hold "until later". When exactly "later" will be remains undefined. Hence it's only the pressure of an approaching deadline, or the wrath of an editor that finally gets the writer moving, and even then only by fits and starts.

The question "What needs to be done now?" will come to our rescue.

To ask the question in the most effective way, we need to tie it into the project statement by putting an "if" before our statement of intention.

So "I am going to write a 2,000 word chapter for Judy Barber's book by 6th December" becomes:

"If I am going to write a 2,000 word chapter for Judy Barber's book by 6 December, underline what needs to be done now?"

One way of getting one's thinking going in the right direction is to phrase the question so as to cover the opposite of the desired result. For instance, "If I'm going to miss Judy's deadline so that she will have to chase me for weeks before I produce a 2,000 word chapter in a rush, what needs to be done now?"

To which the answers might be something like:

- Worry about how I'm going to get it done, rather than work out when I'm going to do it.
- Put off deciding on the subject matter until the deadline is too close to write the chapter in time.
- Avoid considering what the effect on my other work is going to be.
- Take on some more projects to make absolutely certain that I don't have time to do it.
- Avoid at all costs scheduling time for it into my diary.

By doing the opposite to this, we can make some useful decisions, which focus attention on the result, when it's to be done by and what action needs to be taken now to ensure that result by the given date.

My own answers to the question, "If I am going to write a 2,000 word chapter for Judy Barber's book by 6 December, what needs to be done now?" were these:

- Decide on the subject for the chapter
- Obtain agreement to the subject
- Estimate how many days I would need to work on the chapter (Answer: four)
- Schedule in a four-day period during which I would work on the chapter

- Keep reviewing my workload to see if the chapter writing can be brought forward or has to be put back.

Note that when I said I would take four days to write the chapter, I didn't mean that I would do nothing else those days. I meant that I would work on the chapter first thing on each of those days. The chapter actually took me five days, but that didn't worry me as I still had plenty of time until the deadline.

As you read this you may be saying to yourself, "So what's so difficult about writing a chapter?" But that's really the point – there is nothing in the least difficult about writing a chapter – yet huge numbers of people have trouble with doing something as simple as delivering a chapter, an essay or a report by the deadline.

The most common problem that people have with taking action is that they have no system in place for taking on new work. In fact they often don't have any system in place for handling the work they *currently* have. So decisions to take action have a habit of getting lost.

In the above example it was a great help that I was feeding the project into an existing system for dealing with projects. They go in a queue to be actioned one at a time. That way I can see exactly the present state of my workload and my estimates of when it will be done. Without some such system in place, taking on new projects is always going to be a problem area. The good coach will help their clients construct such a system if it doesn't already exist.

Andrea asked herself the question: "If I am going to have my ideal balance of clients in six months' time, what needs to be done now?"

Her answers were as follows:

- Schedule in two days in which to plan my campaign
- Schedule in a period once a week to revise my plans
- Work out what is best done by me and what is best done by other people

By making sure she introduced the project properly in this way, and continuing to ask herself, "What needs to be done now?" she was able to lay the foundations for a successful campaign to get the right balance of clients.

About the Author

Mark Forster is an author and speaker specialising in time management and personal organisation. He has written two books: *Get Everything Done and Still Have Time to Play* and *How to Make Your Dreams Come True.* He believes that most of the traditional time management advice is worse than useless, and has developed his own far more effective methods which focus on getting everything done. He runs frequent very reasonably-priced seminars to teach these methods.

According to the *Independent on Sunday,* Mark is among the Top Ten Life Coaches in the United Kingdom. He has been frequently featured in the media, including whole-page articles about his coaching in the *Observer,* the *Daily Mail* and *The Times.*

He produces a popular free weekly newsletter which contains articles on his latest thinking about coaching and time management. You can subscribe to at his website www.markforster.net which also contains a selection of some of his best articles.

Judy Barber

WHAT HAPPENED?

BY DAVID URE

First I'll tell you why I think "What happened?" is *the* question. Life is constituted by the events that happen to people and then the realm of interpretation they bring to those events. What stops people being effective, having power, being free and being happy – which they are naturally able to be – is living inside an interpretation or decision about their past that they bring into the present and the future. So when somebody is stuck and I'm coaching them, the question I always ask is "What happened?"

The first answer they give is usually not what happened. It is usually inside the realm of interpretation or story or drama that they are re-entering because that is where they are stuck. You have to work at it and keep asking: "What happened? What happened? What happened?" Then you get to what actually happened in reality. Everything that exists in reality exists in a place and at a time and it comes down to a physical event that happened. After that the person gets stuck, which inevitably happens. In the moment of the event happening *they* made a decision and that decision is now the way reality occurs to them. In other words, they confuse the decision with the facts and live inside their own interpretation of the experience. They live in a reality that is a result of their decision and not of the event. Whatever decision they make though is going to limit them. Even if they make what people would think of as a positive decision it is still limiting because they are then no longer present to reality moment by moment.

When people answer the question "What happened?" they immediately see for themselves that what they are stuck with is not what they think they have been stuck with. It's not an issue of reality; it's an interpretation that they are living inside of and when they see that they can continue to live inside that interpretation or they can invent a new one. Then anything becomes possible in that person's life, because we can all choose at any moment to live inside any interpretation at all. None of us are stuck with any of them.

I recall in the Landmark Forum coaching a man who had been an incredibly successful professional athlete. He had won world titles.

His issue was experiencing that he and his wife had "fallen out of love with each other." No matter what he did, from buying flowers to taking her to dinner, nothing seemed to work and there was an absence of romance. He was totally at a loss about what to do so I asked the question, "What happened?" First he told me what people usually do tell me, which was a series of events. I kept on asking, "What happened?" until I got back to the first event. It was the first experience of no romance and no love. As with most people, when he actually saw it, it was both shocking and wonderful.

When they had started their relationship they were on fire with each other. They were in love, staying up late every night at great restaurants drinking champagne. Then he'd compete the next day and he'd win because he was so filled up with the joy of life and he was unstoppable. Then one night, after an event, he reached over and stroked her shoulder and she said: "I don't want to. I've got a headache." That's all that happened. In that moment though he decided: "She is no longer attracted to me." and he spent years living inside that decision, building more and more evidence to support it. When he saw that he realised it was just a momentary decision and that, in reality, it wasn't the case. The moment he let it go he was back in love with his wife and surprisingly, or not, she was back in love with him. Why? Because when you don't live inside the interpretation: "She doesn't love me." you begin to notice all the evidence that leads to the conclusion: "She does love me."

When I was leading the Landmark Forum in Kenya the biggest complaint people had was financial hardship and poverty. One man talked about what really upset him, which was that he worked from sun up to sunset labouring for about a dollar a day. It was barely enough for his family to survive. He considered that his employer was mean – a tyrant who was abusing him. I didn't coach him but he responded to, "What happened?" by sharing a story about a day when he had started work and his employer said something to him. From that small event he made the decision that his employer was a tyrant. In fact it wasn't the money or the working hours that was upsetting him; it was his own decision. After he realised that, he saw that everybody around him worked pretty much the same hours for the same amount of money. It was just the way it was.

He realised that he wasn't being true anymore in having to complain about his bad conditions, so he looked at what he was going to do with his life. He took the money he had put together, which was about twenty five dollars, and he bought some things and started a store. He started his own business. When he shared that the other people saw it. It opened their eyes up to the fact that everybody has got the circumstances and conditions they have. Everybody can get into an agreement based on reality, saying: "We really don't have money. We really are poor." Then what people saw is: "We've got the amount of money we have and so does everybody else. Now we have choices about what we do with it and how we live our lives."

If you talked to the seven or eight thousand people who have attended the Landmark Forum in Kenya then you'd find that most of their circumstances haven't changed. They earn the same amount of money and live in the same, what you or I would consider to be horrendous, conditions but they are happy because they have lived with their choices in life. I see that as a real transformation. It is transforming for a group of people to be able to recognise that they are not trapped inside their circumstances, without deluding themselves by having rose-coloured glasses. They see they have choices and they can make choices.

I led a number of Landmark Forums in Uganda in the early 1990's and many of the people there had lived through the time when Idi Amin had broken Uganda. They had experienced really horrendous things. On the second day of the Landmark Forum I coached a woman and I could tell she was really stuck in her life. She had no joy. She wasn't appreciating life. She couldn't see the point, so I asked her "What happened?". As usual I had to go through it a couple of times but with her it was pretty quick and she got back to one event. What happened was that she had seen her husband murdered by the secret police. In the moment she saw it happen she had decided life wasn't worth living. She could not trust people. She had spent the next seven or eight years living inside the decision she had made. What happened was undeniably what happened in reality, but what she'd decided in that moment made her disempowered, unhappy and not free in life.

She realised her belief that she could not trust *all* people was untrue. There may be people who you shouldn't trust and couldn't trust but it wasn't true of *all* people. It certainly wasn't true that life wasn't worth living, even though her husband's murder had been a heartbreaking event for her. She was alive, she had a family, she had children, she had friends and in that moment she literally snapped out of it. She started breathing differently. Her body and face relaxed visibly. When people see the decision they have been living inside of their physical experience of life alters. They see things differently, they hear things differently and the whole world opens up.

I'll tell you another story because I know you are interested in the leaders and the coaches themselves. I'll give you one from my own life when I considered myself to be an intellectual. I had an honours degree in philosophy – Eastern philosophy and Western philosophy – my life was pretty much devoted to that pathway. I had this whole area of life I did not express myself in which was being physical. Then in the Landmark Forum I saw this man talking. Physically he was in great shape and at the same time he was a smart intelligent person. In that moment I saw that I had the world divided into two types of people, intellectuals and non-intellectuals, and only if you are not intellectual are you physical. I suddenly realised that it came from something really simple.

When I was about 14 years old I was sitting watching a film of the Olympics. In the film they showed the Marathon and in it was this Tanzanian runner, John Stephen Ahkwari, 1968 Mexico. He tripped and fell at the start of the race, getting badly injured. He was advised to pull out and he made what became a famous statement. He said, "My country didn't send me here to not run in the marathon. They sent me here to run." He ran over 26 miles dragging one leg behind him. When I was 14 years old it was the most inspiring thing I had seen in my life. I cried my eyes out and I decided I was going to be an Olympic Marathon runner. The next week I went in the school long distance run and, unfortunately for me, the only training I did was watching that movie. But you know when you are that age you let yourself be inspired. I was inspired so I ran as hard as I could for 400 yards, got a couple of hundred yards ahead of everyone else and thought, "This is going to work!" Then I headed up a hill and couldn't breathe. I stopped, and as the other boys ran past laughing at me, I made a simple decision: "I'm not an athlete." I lived inside that for nine years. Then sitting there in the Landmark Forum I realised it wasn't true. Nobody is an athlete or not an athlete. It's just a decision you make. After that I started running marathons and I still do. I have a physical expression I was never going to have.

Why I think "What happened?" is such a key coaching question is that it gets you present to what's running your life. When you realise that what's running your life is a series of decisions you can then choose to make new ones. The ones that limit you are the ones that got made up in moments of upset or stress. In those moments of upset and stress they may even have been the right decisions. If there's a bus coming towards me and I'm sitting in the road and I decide to jump out of the way that's probably the right decision to make. If I then spend the rest of my life being jumpy and avoiding buses when I'm not in front of a bus that's silly and disempowering.

Look beyond that. People are powerful. People are smart. People are courageous. People are capable of great joy and great peacefulness. And there is part of the mechanism we're given that we all have to deal with all the time which is automatically interpreting and making things mean something. We are making decisions and not noticing we're doing it. So with the question "What happened?" I'm guiding people to start to living a life in which they begin to notice their own machinery. You can notice your own interpretations and you can take them straight out. You can start to live your life moment to moment being present and when you are present to life itself anything is possible.

The facts are the facts and things are the way they are, but that's never what determines how people experience life, even if they have money and a great environment. I have just been to Australia. They have a great environment and yet still people complain about it. Why? They are not present. They could be in central London in a little bed-sit and be happy. When I'm present anything is possible. I can create my life.

I watch my twenty month old son and he wakes up every morning excited. That's vision for me, the excitement of being alive and of thinking "Something is possible. What am I going to create?" I think people naturally have vision. I don't try to get them to create a vision until they've had a chance to take away the layers of interpretation they've had and the decisions they made in moments of upset. Then they naturally get returned to their current childlike state of innocence, grace and lightness. When they are there they will create something that is just right for them.

About the Author

David Ure is General Manger for Landmark Education in Europe and a successful senior Landmark Forum Leader. He was born and raised in Melbourne, Australia where he received his BA in philosophy at Melbourne University. Philosophy fascinated and inspired him. His passion was, and is, having really intense conversations. His life was heading towards lecturing in philosophy when a close friend urged him to attend a Landmark Education seminar. At first he resisted her enthusiasm, but it was contagious and he went along. After tying himself in his own favourite kinds of philosophical knots, and hearing new questions, he realised in the Landmark Forum that he had come home.

In a year he had done every programme they offered in Australia, was a much happier man, and knew he wanted to lead Landmark Education programmes. Since then he has been extensively trained in delivering the programmes and "technology" powerfully and effectively. In the last 12 years, he has led courses for more than 45,000 individuals in 17 countries. David consistently achieves the highest ratings from individuals, organisations, and groups for his presentation and delivery of Landmark Education's unique programmes.

David Ure is one of just over 50 programme leaders in this global training and development company offering unique educational programmes creating breakthrough results for people and organisations. The programmes allow people to produce concrete results in their effectiveness, impacting important areas of life such as career, relationships, and productivity.

David is humbled by the privilege of working in an enterprise committed to the fundamental principle that people have the possibility of success, fulfilment, and greatness.

David Ure currently leads the Landmark Forum, the three and a half day core programme, and others offered by Landmark Education in London and around the world.

www.landmarkeducation.com

PART TWO: THINKING MODELS FOR MOVING TOWARDS SUCCESS

The writers in this group use thinking models to present ideas clearly. Some of these are models they have created themselves. Models can give structure to our thinking and to coaching and are good tools for remembering concepts. Deepak Lodhia's model aims towards a goal, Ewemade Orobator uses a ladder to success, David Hyner projects a line into the future, Gary Outrageous uses a scale of one to a hundred to check motivation and Julie French uses a pyramid of neurological levels to consider different approaches to problem-solving. But as you'll see, the models are only part of what they do and write about, and all are encouraging people to succeed.

How can you use thinking models to help you move forward?

Judy Barber

WHAT'S YOUR AIM IN LIFE?

BY DEEPAK LODHIA

Have you ever been asked the question, "What's your aim in life?"

Have you ever understood what the person asking the question meant?

It's quite a powerful question because it is a pretty direct and incisive way to ascertain what your purpose in life is and what you aim to achieve as a goal.

For most people it is quite challenging to define one's life with a single answer, especially since the first time you hear a question like this you may be only ten or fifteen years old.

The first time I heard this question I was twelve years old and was asked this by my mathematics teacher. I replied, "Sorry sir, I don't quite understand the question." At which point he retorted, "Are you stupid boy? What do you want to do when you grow up?"

Clearly to my old maths teacher the question was all about what career path you wish to follow when you get older, probably because that was important to him. Recently I heard the same question posed to a colleague of mine. She elicited a whole list of goals and "wants" for the coming years, so in her case the question was about achievement through goal attainment.

At this point, I decided to take this questioning further and to break down the question further to create a better understanding. What I created has become known as the "Lodhia Model". Take a piece of paper and pen and follow this through to see what comes up for you.

What is your AIM in life? Or should I say what is your:

Awareness

Intention

Motion through emotion, in life?

Right now, what is your Awareness?

...

Right now, what are your Intentions?

...

Right now, what is your Motion through emotion?

...

"What?" I hear you say. Let's take each of these in turn so I can explain.

What Is Your Awareness?

They say awareness changes everything, and only when you become aware can you change anything. So, start to pay attention to everything. What I mean by this is pay 100% attention to everything around you and start to notice what you notice. Your awareness will give you very specific clues as to where you are in life right now. If you don't pay attention, the clues may come like feathers, like a brick or even a truck. But if you pay attention right now in this moment, be honest, what is your awareness telling you right now?

Does answering the question make you feel quite tense or more relaxed?

If it makes you feel tense, is it possible that your awareness is telling you to dig deeper? Or maybe to be more honest with yourself?

When you truly listen to your awareness, you may notice that you feel more relaxed throughout the body. Even your mind may become quieter over time. The key is to pay attention 100%.

So, may I ask you as you listen to your awareness, where are you at right now in life?

Remember there is no right or wrong answer; this is just what you perceive right now, so just allow yourself to be as specific as you want.

What Are Your Intentions?

Before I launch into intention, which I believe is a whole topic of study in itself, may I ask you this question?

What is the difference between 'want' and 'intention'?

Would you care to try an exercise to help illustrate the difference?

WANTS AND INTENTIONS

Take a piece of paper and a pen. Divide the piece of paper into two columns. In the left hand column write "Wants" and write down everything you want in life. Be as extravagant as you like. Imagine it's your birthday and really go for it! Now in the right column write "Intentions" and write down all the things that you intend to do.

Once you have finished, notice the difference between the two columns. What do you notice?

You may find that the list on the right is much shorter and a lot more specific. This is because your conscious mind and subconscious mind have to work together to design an intention rather than to just dream up ideas. Your awareness now holds you to account on what you believe to be possible right now! Intentions also have to be in line with values and beliefs. This is why intentions are more powerful, even in language, try it. Say I want .... (fill in the gap), now say I intend to get .... (fill in the gap). Just notice the difference in your physiology and subconscious determination by making a small adjustment to a simple statement.

Try this exercise. Make a list of all your intentions, every single one. Now go back and look at your awareness about each intention.

Is it truly what you intend? Be specific. Do the same process again until it is true for you. Then ask yourself: "What areas of my life will it impact? And how will it impact my life? Is this what I truly intend?" If it is not truly what you intend then go back and rewrite the intention and do the process again.

By doing this you are breathing life into every intention and translating it from possibility to reality by visualizing each context and area of your life which is affect by the result of your intention.

So, what are your intentions in life?

What is your Motion through emotion?

This is probably the most controversial and yet simple part of my approach. No human being will do anything unless it is emotionally charged. In other words there is no motion without emotion. Let me clarify this. Imagine any goal you want in life. If you achieve it, what will *that* give you? And again what will *that* give you? And again what will *that* give you? In fact, if you keep asking that last question you will always get to an emotion. Everything that we do or that has us behave in a certain way is to do with emotion.

So look at all your intentions, imagine having achieved them, how will that make you feel?

So, why wait? Are you going to put in all that hard work and get to the goal to feel that emotion just for an instant? Then what?

My take on this is different from that of many others. Why not have that emotion all the way from the beginning? Why not have it from the point of awareness to the end when you complete your intention? Why not use that emotion as fuel for the journey to keep you going when you hit a sticky patch or a brick wall? In fact many of my clients have achieved breakthrough results in record time by using this method. So, what is the emotion you are looking to get from your result? How are you going to be being from day to day to make sure you evoke that emotion from within, right now?

In other words, who are you going to be in order to create the results of your intention?

We have looked at each component of the model in a very simple way. The model goes a lot deeper, but understanding the model is not the key here. How you can use this model to create breakthrough results in your life is what is important.

Putting the model back together.

When we follow the exercises we get the following:

- Awareness
    - o   Where are you at, right now?
- Intention
    - o   Where do you intend to be?
- Motion
    - o   What fuel will you use to get there?

Notice that, so far, this model has no action or doing steps. It is all about planning and TAKING AIM! So you could say the original question "What is your aim in life?" is about planning intentional goals for life with the purpose of arriving at them in your own time *and* enjoying the journey. If you want to use the Lodhia Model to achieve goals there are just three steps after the planning and these are as follows:

1.   Make a sequential list of actions to take and when by.

2.   Just in case, prepare for the worst-case scenarios and have contingency plans so you can stop worrying about the problems and then just focus on expecting the best outcomes without attachment.

3.   GO FOR IT, take actions with integrity!

It can be just that simple and easy. What if I told you that you have a choice and you can choose to let it be easy, would you still do it?

I used to be a person who would set a goal for whatever reason but mainly because of the challenge. I would go head first into the project doing action after action, until I had achieved what I set out to achieve. What I found was that I was always emotionally drained and always felt tired. The feeling of achievement was never there. Yes, I accumulated all the material possessions I desired, but no, I didn't feel fulfilled. I was never one for planning: I was a man of action!

Bullshit! I was someone who was running around achieving small goals so I could tick the box and say to myself that I was doing something with my life. It had to be a challenge and nearly wipe me out for me to get a sense of "I did" something.

After spending nearly ten years of my life chasing this idea and noticing that I had not moved any further on I decided to go back and take that long hard look at what my aim in life was! It was at that point I realised that all the clues were around me - Aha! Awareness! In fact about 90% of the goals I had achieved or was fighting to achieve were difficult because they went against my core values. This caused me all kinds of physical and emotional tensions and made the attainment of the goals even harder. This was because, as the laws of the universe dictated, I got exactly what I wanted. Now I get what I intend, because it is absolutely in line with my values and beliefs. That's how it is with intentions.

Better still, I don't have to wait for the intention to be fulfilled for me to feel that buzz of emotion. By choosing who I am being moment to moment, I get to feel that same buzz of emotion everyday without worrying if I achieve the intention or not. The amazing thing is that the more I detach from the intention the more I attract it!

Now I choose MASSIVE goals. I apply my model. I plan my route. I prepare for the worst and expect the best. Then I go for it! I now achieve massive breakthrough goals, bigger than I had ever dreamt possible and I do it with the least amount of effort.

But the best thing with this model is that, whether you achieve the intention or not, you get to live every moment in line with your values and have each moment filled with that sense of fulfilment. My aim in life is to teach every person who wishes to learn how to live in the now, moment by moment and have each moment be in line with their values and with fulfilment. That is my aim in life. I hope you will share yours with me too! Because of this technique the people I work with have become self-empowered: they set bigger goals and achieve them in shorter periods of time. This enables them to have more balanced and fulfilling lives and allows them invest back into society.

If you could achieve more by doing less, what would you give back?

"The soul is dyed the colour of its thoughts. Think only those things that are in line with your principles and bear the light of day. The content of your character is your choice. Day by day, what you choose, what you think and what you do is who you become. Your integrity is your destiny... it is the light that guides your way."

Heraclitus

About the Author

Deepak Lodhia is the Director of Coaching for Prime Source

He originally qualified as a pharmacist and worked in the research sector with a multinational company and then in the retail sector. He discovered his skill in motivating people to excel in work performance and quickly became known as the person to go to for getting things done fast!

Deepak later qualified as a coach with the European Coaching Foundation. His numerous skills and qualifications include NLP, EFT and the Sedona Method and allow him to deliver results quickly and effectively. He is also a qualified firewalk instructor.

Deepak's focuses on helping clients:

- Become self empowered
- Set and achieve bigger goals
- Remove blocks holding them back
- Start living the life of their dreams today
- The practical result is that clients:
  - o Achieve more than they thought themselves capable of
  - o Achieve their goals in less time
  - o Live more balanced and fulfilled lives
  - o Stand out from the crowd

Deepak was head hunted by Prime Source Training because he delivers results for his clients in a fast, effective manner and is passionate about helping people achieve more. His integrity and level of commitment are renowned amongst people fortunate to have him as their coach. He is known for challenging the ordinary to become *extra*ordinary.

Deepak has a unique ability to open people's minds so they think 'outside the box'. He helps people put themselves back in the driving seat of their careers or lives. Deepak has real talent for seeing what is actually going on with people. His intuition and empathy set him apart from most coaches. His commitment to his clients is to support them and help them do whatever it takes to achieve the results they seek. The greatest tribute to Deepak's uniqueness is the number of coaches he coaches. He truly is a Coach's Coach!

You can contact Deepak at:
ww.theprimesource.net / Deepak@theprimesource.net

WHY NOT ME NOW?

BY EWEMADE OROBATOR

ACHIEVING THE NATURAL STATE OF SUCCESS

You would undoubtedly agree that we need the air we breathe and we know that without it we cannot live.

So in true Jackanory style (for those of you who remember those days of yore), let me tell you a story.

Above All Else!

A young boy asked the wise old man of the village to tell him what the secret of success was. He asked, "How can I guarantee that can I have all I want?" The old man simply turned to the boy and said, "Bring some food and water and let us walk." The young boy could not contain himself with excitement for at last he was going to learn the greatest secret of all.

They walked together in silence for a whole day and the boy's curiosity was heightened – was the secret of success then to be silent? Out of respect he was not going to ask lest he be accused of impatience.

This heightened curiosity was replaced by genuine confusion when by the end of the second day the pair had still not exchanged a word and no secret was revealed.

By mid–point during the third day, that initial innocent curiosity that had been replaced by confusion was now in danger of being replaced by incredulity. At that point they came to a lake. For the journey to continue they had to cross the lake. Yet no boat or form of transport was in sight. Undeterred the old man waded into the lake.

The young boy was reassured to see that the lake came no more than half way up the old man and he quickly followed to remain at the old

37

man's side. Whilst it was deeper for the young boy he was not consumed and was able to proceed fairly easily.

However, the feeling of incredulity was now being supplanted by disillusionment. He had followed this man in silence for what seemed like days. He was still none the wiser and now, to make matters worse, he was soaking wet.

Suddenly the old man turned to the young boy and placed his hand on the boy's head. Then, to the boy's complete bewilderment, submerged the boy underneath the water and held him there. At that point the young boy felt that he had been tricked and was facing certain death. The seconds seemed like hours as the old man's grip was like that of a man at his physical prime. Why is the old man trying to kill me? Yet the boy held on to life for at that moment it was all he had. Then, as suddenly as he had plunged the boy under the water, he released him and the boy was free.

As angry as he was, the boy was more grateful for the fresh air that seemed sweeter than ever before. The old man then turned to the gasping boy and said, "My son, when you were under the water what was the most important thing to you?" Even though he was angry and wet, the resentment in the boy's answer was as clear as the cleanest sea, "To breathe you old fool, of course it was to breathe." The old man simply smiled and said...

"When you desire success as badly as you want to breathe you will get it. I just reminded you how much you wanted to breathe. Now show me how badly you desire success."

At that moment, the boy knew he had been taught the most powerful lesson he had ever learnt and he could not believe how short a time it had taken to learn it.

I have always recognised that the world constantly changes and that it is **an absolute myth** to contend with what we cannot change. Further, I recognise change does not occur logically or follow a natural path. It is often erratic, creeping and discontinuous. Within us we must encourage a natural response to these facts and use the phenomena of certain change to ensure personal growth. We must recognise that, with absolute belief and burning desire, possibilities are limitless and defeat is not an option. I know this is true and have used it to achieve exceptional personal, business and social successes.

The Progress Isolators

The power of self-belief and burning desire is at the root of the most successful people in history, bar none – bar absolutely none.

Yet despite this power, too often our dreams are destroyed or damaged by others or by reacting to our perception of the world. I call these causes of damage the Progress Isolators. They are around us everyday. Sometimes other people knowingly cause damage. Most of the time though, our perception of the world and inadequate appreciation of our psyche are sub-conscious. As the world revolves around people, we need to be aware of these people NOW! I am afraid the chances are you have already met them! These instant "experts" are the people who suffocate your ambitions instead of speeding them along. They are ready to douse your fire without an ounce of proper evidence behind them. For example, "I want to start my own business" may meet the reply, "I wouldn't if I were you – look how many people fail..." Or the same proposition may meet with what I call the Sowers of Doubt – "Good on you mate... rather you than me!" or "I wouldn't, but well done for trying."

And what about those who will back you all the way but only back you up with the negative inputs? For example, "Great idea to start a business. You can do it I am certain - but what about... And what if... Not forgetting... and watch out for..."

It is these Progress Isolators that take you away from your natural state because you start to believe and live their myth. You let them into your self-esteem and you let them destroy your world. Why is that? In which name do they do this? Which superior motivating force more powerful than burning desire and self-belief do they call upon in order to let them sway you?

If you took your place, your natural place of success, and everyone in society did too – what would it be like? Instead of having a society where we trust others to abuse our lives for their own ends, we would have an honest society with empowered individuals able to work for the collective good without being reliant on external authorities to lead them. We would find our own remedies for the most serious problems in the world – poverty, disease, ignorance, war etc... We would not rely on these external authorities that year after year fail to deliver but continue to ask us to trust them. We would have empowered individuals who would use their individual faith and beliefs in whatever form they take to look into their soul and unleash its full potential. What problem in the world could withstand that? Absolutely none.

Returning To The Natural State of Success

To return to a natural state of success may involve us, at first, having a constant inner battle so that when a new possibility arises, when a call to action is needed, we must conquer the voice of doubt and inhibition, and repeat to ourselves again and again that *it can be done.*

The voice of doubt and inhibition is the most powerful inner input we have and one we cannot shut out. It so often controls us and we do not control its entry. I am talking about the voice inside our heads. No greater authority exists than the spoken voice and when it is inside our head, it can be omnipotent. So when the voice asks "Why?" – you can reply "Why not?" and you can add "Why not me?" before finally adding "Why not me now?"

Returning to a natural state of success demands that we take full responsibility for what happens to us. We dismiss the notion of fate and we resolve to map out our own life plan. We realise that everything in this world is ours if we truly want it, as I have described, as naturally as breathing air. We must abandon the haven of dependence for independence. That does not mean we work in isolation but that we work together with people committed to the goals we believe in - people who will only act as a positive injection into our life and the dreams we have. There is no room for doubt, defeat or apathy - that is what is required to return to the natural state of success.

Just imagine the state of a psyche free from doubt, fear, inhibition and defeat. Imagine what you would do if you knew failure was not an option. Imagine a world where the possibilities before you were as endless as the wind and as vast as the deserts. You do not have to go too far to imagine this erstwhile natural state because... you were there as a child.

Being in this state, you will enjoy at least one or more of the core values every single one of us desires. These core values that drive our needs are obtainable, if you want it badly enough and believe, truly believe that you can have it. What are the core values that unite the billions of people in the world? I challenge you to tell me if at least one of your core values are here in this list and I challenge you to spot one that I have not mentioned.

- excellent mental and physical health
- loving relationships
- material wealth
- inner peace
- personal and spiritual development

So am I right? Billions and billions of people in the world are driven by the same basic values? Incredible but true.

It is simply a matter of letting yourself succeed. It is a matter of getting out of your own way. Why is it that we succeed by adopting a certain set of principles to achieve a certain result but do not apply a similar set of principles (of course not necessarily similar actions) to achieve similar results in areas of our life that have been unsuccessful? It remains one of the great mysteries of humanity and perhaps led to the famous saying that *"The definition of insanity is doing the same thing the same way and expecting different results!"*

The Secret of Success

One of the great eccentricities of man is our capacity to reinvent the wheel. No, not make it better, faster, last longer etc. but simply to plain re-invent it. Why do we do that? Imagine you made something. It has taken burning desire and self-belief, years of effort, trial and error, persistence, determination and pain to get to the result you were sure to get. Then what do you do? Celebrate as you should? No? We often do not even do a little thing like celebrate. No, of course not, the best thing to do is to start all over again and try and invent the same thing! Go through all the burning desire, self-belief, years of effort... Just to invent the same thing again. Pure madness you would agree. Yet we do it everyday. We believe that success is unique and cannot be guaranteed unless we do it our way. After all, who else knows about that unique product or service you want to offer?

So just to ensure the avoidance of any doubt, can I say as clearly and as loudly as I possibly can and as persistently as I possibly can that:

> **The secret of success has already been invented.**
> **Do not waste time trying to invent it again – just**
> **copy it and follow it every day of your life.**

That is right – someone has already found it. Sorry, and no there is not a better way or faster way or unique way of ensuring success. There is and has only ever been one way to guarantee success – the right way. The amazing thing is it was invented many, many ages ago. I always wanted someone to give me a leg up to find success, so here you are, a ladder that is not very long, but one that you must climb each day, religiously. You will get to the top.

The Ladder of Success

Reached the top? Head towards new goals
and climb a new ladder of success.

SUSTAIN YOUR ACHIEVEMENT

Perseverance!

CELEBRATE YOUR ACHIEVEMENTS

REVIEW YOUR PROGRESS

FEED YOUR VISION

You may have
to lose those
you love or
things you like.

BUILD YOUR SUPPORT TEAM

THE PAIN OF CHOICE

BURNING DESIRE

SELF-BELIEF

COMMIT TO ACT DAILY

WRITE THEM DOWN

SET YOUR GOALS

In summary, returning to a natural state of success is what can be yours and I hope this chapter in Judy's book has helped you to move towards that. "Why not me now?" is a question that you can use to open up the possibility of success. It isn't an elusive secret that takes learning a lot or being someone special. Good luck every time you climb the ladder and help others to climb it.

About the Author

Ewemade Orobator is Director of Operations at Entrepreneurs in Action Ltd. This is a coaching and support organisation that has so far helped over 3,000 young learners and adults to develop their enterprise awareness and business ideas.

His publication as Co-author of Living an Extraordinary Life was released in the United States, Canada and Britain in August 2001.

His media appearances include live interviews on BBC local radio and in BBC programmes such as the Daily Politics.

He is also President of the Black and Minority Television, Film and Media Charitable Foundation that has set up an Internet Television Channel, www.bmetv.net that is now broadcasting on a platform accessible by 680 million homes around the world.

He can be contacted on: ewemade007@btinternet.com

WHAT IF I DO NOTHING?

BY DAVID HYNER

When working with clients I help them to see how they can achieve MASSIVE goals as opposed to the much taught realistic and achievable goals.

Before I do this though I use a tool to help clients see the folly of not taking positive action towards achieving their goal.

I call it the **'Line Of Consequence'**.

By using this clients can easily demonstrate to themselves how doing nothing will have a massive negative impact on their life or career, thus leaving them with only one realistic option – to take positive action.

I get people to draw a line down the page with spaces (like rungs on a ladder) up and down the line.

I then ask them to imagine that they are in the present situation in the middle of this line. If they take no positive action, what are the consequences to their life, job, health, finances, family etc?

For example – "I want to run a marathon. If I take no action, what are the consequences?"

Answers could include – not getting fit, feeling like a failure, loss of credibility etc.

They write this on the first rung or space down.

If that happens, what is the consequence of this, and so on down the ladder.

For example – "If I lose credibility, what are the consequences?"

Answers could include – guilt, shame, anger, frustration etc.

"If I feel frustration, what are the consequences?"

Answers could include – stress, anxiety, ill health, lack of effectiveness etc.

... and so on down the ladder until they see that this is a BAD place to go and surely taking no action is not an option.

I then say, "What if you do take positive action right now?"

They write this consequence on the first rung *up* the ladder.

What if they then take more action? – what would be the consequence of that?... and so on until they can see the real benefits of taking action now.

The consequence of change is there for all to see, but most of us do not take action in a positive way. In fact we often take little or no action and end up with the same mediocre results that we always get or, worse still, our results deteriorate.

Choose to, "Go up the ladder, not down."

A recent example of how I used this model was during a charity event for Wonder Years Centre of Excellence (www.wonderyearsce.co.uk).

This amazing British charity works out in the Gambia helping to create the sustainable development of a whole community through the provision of education, healthcare, economic and skills development.

I was part of a dynamic group of volunteers who spent time living and working with villagers to learn from each other and to help the charity bring about positive change within a village called Medina Salaam.

Life is fragile, and often short, in the Gambia due to health challenges, lack of infrastructure, lack of jobs and lack of education. So, understandably, there is a "general" short-term vision amongst its people.

To plan for weeks, months or years in advance is perceived by many as a futile exercise as for most (in rural communities) the day to day task of survival can take up much of their time and energy. Money, jobs and in some cases – food – are hard to come by.

A Personal Library

During a conversation with one of the English speaking and educated men in the village (and at his request) I ventured to understand one of his challenges and tried to offer a new perspective.

This example and the following one are based upon true past situations whilst the names or exact terms of reference have been altered to protect people's privacy.

The conversation went something like this...

"What is it you would like to happen?"

"What I would dearly love is my own library with very good books that I can learn from and then share that knowledge with others in our village but I can never afford this."

"Do you know that to be true or is that a belief?"

"Yes. It is true. How can I possibly afford to buy books?"

"Would you like to look into how maybe you could get your books?"

"Oh yes... That would be very good."

"Okay... I see that you smoke."

"Yes I smoke."

"How many cigarettes do you smoke each day?"

"I don't know, it depends what I can afford."

"Approximately?"

"About 5 but sometimes 10"

"Okay... and how much does that cost you?"

"50 Delasi."

"Okay ... how much would it cost to buy your first ten books?"

"About 3000 Delasi I guess."

"Good... so let's do a line of consequence."

"What is that?"

"Have a look at this"

I then drew a line in the dirt with a stick and drew a stick man in the middle of the line. I worked down and then up the line asking the "consequence question at each stage. Like this...

"You are here okay?"

"Okay"

"You are an educated man so tell me what will happen if you continue to smoke for the rest of your life?"

"It will cost me lots of money and I'll get ill... Maybe."

"Okay... if that happens, what are the consequences to you and your family of you losing money and/or getting ill?"

"Ohhhh... that would be very bad indeed. We are very poor so my family would go hungry if my children could not work and I cannot afford the cost of medicine."

"If your family went hungry and you could not afford medicine, what are the consequences to you and your family?"

"Ohhhh... that would be very bad. I do not want to say."

"Okay... So perhaps smoking is not a good idea?"

"No... but it is hard to stop."

"What could motivate you to stop?"

"What do you mean?"

I now start to work *up* the line asking the consequence question at each stage. Like this...

"If you were to stop smoking what would the consequence be?"

"Ah! I would have more money and maybe not get ill?"

"Yes... good... and if you say had more money... what would be the direct consequence to you being able to afford medicine or perhaps buy yourself your first book?"

"Ohhhhhh yes, that would be very good indeed."

"What would a consequence be?"

"If I stopped buying cigarettes and saved the money I would quickly be able to buy my first book"

"Excellent! How would that make you feel?"

"I would be very happy!"

"If you stop smoking, save the money, and buy your first book, what is a consequence of that happening?"

"I would be very proud."

"If you are reading your book and sharing the education that you have from the book, what is a consequence of that happening?"

At this point, he sat upright and beamed a smile from ear to ear as understanding and acceptance lit up his face.

Nothing more was said until that evening when he called me over to where he was sitting. His smile was a picture.

"I have stopped smoking!"

"Fantastic!"

Time will tell if this man gets his library, but we worked out that if he stops smoking for three years and spends the money on books, he would have a library that would make him one of the proudest men in Gambia.

The awareness that a belief is not always the truth, can be hard to swallow at times: we rely a lot on our belief systems and it can take a lot to overcome our emotional ties to them.

But it can also be liberating, motivating and inspiring when we learn that many of our limiting beliefs are not in fact based upon truth or fact, but on misguided opinions.

Using the line of consequence, it is very quick and easy to discover if what you're doing is going to have positive or negative consequences in the future.

Then the decision to make a change or not is often a lot easier.

Here's another example...

Back On Top

G had been long term unemployed after being made redundant despite being a top performer at national level within his organisation.

G felt that his confidence had been shattered and over time, despite being a very pleasant, hard working and honest man, found that in an interview situation, he became a nervous shadow of his real self.

I worked with G through the line of consequence.

The conversation went something like this...

"What is it you would like to happen?"

"I just want to work and earn a living for my own self respect."

"Would you like to look into how maybe you could make a change?"

"Yeah, cool."

"Okay... What are the consequences of you not getting a job?"

"Relying on benefits for the rest of my life, but I don't want that."

"Why not?"

"There are things I want to do in my life and I am sick of having no money and no self respect."

"If you do not get a job that you like that is good for you then what are the consequences of having no money and losing your self respect?"

"I'll get depressed and feel down I suppose?"

"What are the consequences of you getting depressed?"

"I could get really low and maybe think about topping myself."

G gave an uneasy smirk as he realised that while he said the words casually, and in a "matter of fact" tone, that the reality could be just that – a reality.

"A bad thing?"

"Yeah – a very bad thing."

"Okay... So let's look at what happens if you go up the line shall we?"

"Yes but getting a job when you have been unemployed for five years or more is not that easy."

"What could motivate you to 'have to' get a job?"

"What do you mean?"

"Is contemplating topping yourself an option for you?"

"No way!"

I now start to work up the line asking the consequence question at each stage. Like this...

"If you were to get a good job, what would the consequence be?"

"Money, pride, respect, belief, confidence..."

"If you got a job and got more – let's say – confidence back then what would be a direct consequence to you?"

"If I was more confident and had money I would buy some football boots and go back to being a referee at weekends. I really used to love that."

"Good – okay – what would a consequence be of you having a job, some money to buy boots and going back to being a referee in your spare time?"

"I would be made up. That would be so good."

(The smile was there already)

"Excellent! How would that make you feel?"

"I'm excited at the thought of it. I can't stop smiling."

"What would happen if you got excited and smiled a lot?"

"I would... Yeah – okay – I get it now!"

"Is not getting a job an option?"

"No way... I have to get a job."

"Okay... What will stop you?"

"Nothing. I have to do this."

G managed to borrow some football boots and started to referee the very next weekend.

Within weeks he had a job. Not an ideal job, but one that he said helped to give him confidence to go on and look for an even better job and to know that it was "down to him".

Use this model for your own challenges and to help others to work through their challenges, and always remember to question if what you or they believe to be true is based upon fact or fiction.

Go for it!

Nobody decides what you are capable of achieving except you, so take action – TODAY!

"The Line of Consequence"

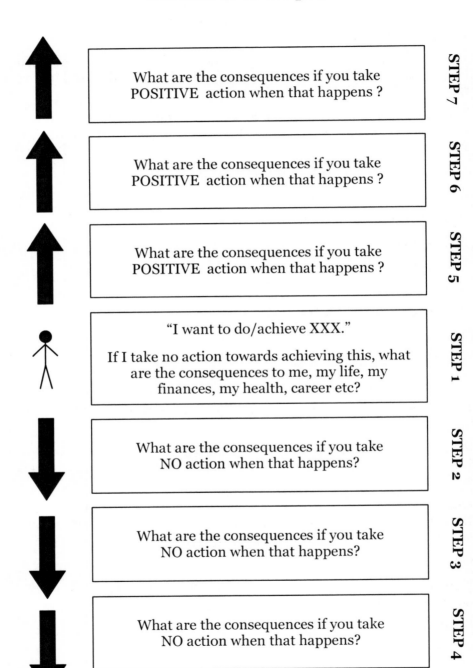

STEP 7

What are the consequences if you take POSITIVE action when that happens ?

STEP 6

What are the consequences if you take POSITIVE action when that happens ?

STEP 5

What are the consequences if you take POSITIVE action when that happens ?

STEP 1

"I want to do/achieve XXX."

If I take no action towards achieving this, what are the consequences to me, my life, my finances, my health, career etc?

STEP 2

What are the consequences if you take NO action when that happens?

STEP 3

What are the consequences if you take NO action when that happens?

STEP 4

What are the consequences if you take NO action when that happens?

About the Author

David Hyner, is an acclaimed International speaker, trainer and researcher in the field of achievement and personal effectiveness. He has a LAMDA Diploma and gold medal in Public Speaking.

David is listed in the pages of the International Book of Who's Who.

David has spent many years conducting research interviews with many top achievers including sports stars, captains of industry, scientists, entrepreneurs, inventors, explorers, politicians and entertainers.

This research has developed into unique, inspiring, highly motivational and effective keynote speeches, one-to-one coaching and training workshops.

His speciality is in helping people to find their purpose in life and business, and then apply themselves in ways that mirror the thoughts, actions and behaviours of the world's top achievers.

David applies this training to his own development and has used his unique goal setting model to break the fundraising records of 4 charities and organised one event alone that raised £288,000 in his spare time for Cancer Research UK.

David is regional vice-president of the Midlands PSA (professional speakers association) and delivers research based training in the following areas:

- The MASSIVE Goal Principle – NOT realistic & achievable goals!
- Get InCredible Sales - a new look at sales training.
- Stress Prevention – NOT stress management!
- Inside The Minds of Top Achievers – Look into, NOT up to!
- Inspiring Presentations – 24 top tips for inspired public speaking!
- The Work/Life See-Saw – Control it before it controls you!

Learn more at...

www.stretchdevelopment.com / www.davidhyner.com

Judy Barber

WHO IS THIS 'SOMEONE'? WHICH OF YOUR GOALS DO YOU WANT MOST? AND, ON A SCALE OF ONE TO A HUNDRED, WHERE IS THIS ON YOUR WANTON DESIRE SCALE?

BY GARY OUTRAGEOUS

I'm going to tell you something about how I work, my own visions and goal, and about three of the questions I use when working with visions and goals.

I work a lot speaking to large groups as well as one to one. I provoke people with questions to get feedback. In the first few minutes I want energy, feedback and people talking. I don't want to be lecturing because that's not my style. I can lecture if they want, but I find that interaction gets people thinking and helps the learning. The key is getting people to take action!

I ask the audience "Can you remember the first time you tried to ride a bike?" And most go "yes". Then I ask what happened. They say ... "I fell off." and my next question is, "What did you do next?" Again they reply, "I fell off." and again I ask them, ""What did you do next?" They say, "I fell off again." By the way, this is leading somewhere...

I then ask "What did you do next?" again because I want to get them annoyed with me. If I irritate them a bit I'll get them to remember something. What I am aiming at is that when we are children we don't believe in the concept of failure because we don't know what it is. We know when something is not working, but that's different. We don't know we've failed.

The time when we begin to understand failure is when we go to school. Some well-meaning teacher, who in all fairness is doing their job, talks about success and failure with a tick and a cross. That's when it all starts. The teacher becomes a 'someone'. Before then you just fell off your bike and you got back on again. Nothing stopped you from doing the thing you wanted to do most which was learning to ride your bike.

Visions and Goals

I want to do various things and I'll share some of them with you because they relate to my questions. I have big visions and particular goals.

- A main vision is sharing the use of 21st century hypnosis for people to get what they truly want. I am a business hypnotist. Another way to put that is that I want to be the person who cleans the windows in peoples' lives and shows them how to clean windows themselves. It was Plato who said, "You cannot teach a man anything; you can only help him to find it within himself."

- Another big vision is standing on stage and spreading the "good word." That is that... everyone makes decisions based on "wanton desire". The reason why they change their life is desire – a desire to be somewhere else rather than where they are now.

- One vision I had was for a sales and marketing club to help people who are stuck get unstuck. This is now set up and is beginning to grow!

- Our family goal is to move to a Greek island. We visualise this one on a daily basis and then let it go. This is our main goal for ourselves that influences all the other goals and it's important that we are aware it is our main goal. I'll explain that later.

I also have the important vision of helping people tap in to the fact that life isn't difficult. It isn't difficult to reach your goals. For instance, if you were in India, would you meet a tiger that needs coaching on how to be a tiger? Tigers like that don't exist.

We've lost our ability to tap into intuition and nature. Sales and marketing is so simple and people try and make it difficult so they can charge people loads of money to learn about it. They try and make it difficult because they think they are being intellectual, but I would rather imagine a puma. When she is sitting there looking at her prey she will glisten and all she will be is a puma.

It is about being real, being honest, knowing who you are, knowing what you want and going for it without harming others. It is just honestly thinking 'This is what I truly want.' and not being embarrassed, ashamed or made to feel guilty because of opinions based on what *'someone'* thinks. That way I think you are more likely to realise your visions for helping other people as well.

Rooting out the 'Someone' Syndrome!

I can't stand the 'someone' syndrome. It's about *someone*, somewhere saying that what you want to achieve or have is bad. My response to that is... "Who is this 'Someone'?". It's a great coaching question. That voice could be from the newspapers such as The Sun or it could be the Guardian. It could be a news reporter. It could be anyone. There's always *Someone!*

The trick is catching yourself. It's normally in conversation when you are chatting away and all of a sudden you find yourself saying "Oh, someone said recently..."

In that moment you need to have some sort of alarm bell ringing. You need to be asking yourself: "Is this true? Have I just read this somewhere and am I sure it is true?"

It's important to be ready with a "Someone Syndrome" detector when somebody uses "Someone" on you, and not to be affected by it. The best way to be inoculated against the "Someone Syndrome" is by asking, "Who specifically said that?" This question clears the clutter. It "Feng Shui's" the conversation!

You could say it's a conversational Feng Shui technique... "Who specifically said that? When did they say it? Why did they say that? Are you sure they said that?" Nine times out of ten this "Someone" is a figment of the imagination or a distortion of the facts.

Someone said in 2002 that there were weapons of mass destruction in Iraq!

Someone said that in 45 minutes Saddam Hussein could get those weapons ready and launch them. Look what happened as a result of the Someone Syndrome there. We went to war with a country, rightly or wrongly, without knowing the truth of what someone said. That's the power of the Someone Syndrome. It's a way of abdicating responsibility. "Ah well, it must be ok because someone said it or someone did it."

In his book "Influence", Robert Cialdini talks about social proof. He discusses a murder where there were many witnesses to a woman being put through hell by her boyfriend. When they were interviewed those people, who heard the woman being attacked said: "We thought someone else would have reported it." It seems that if you've got loads of witnesses you've got less chance of being helped than if there's only a few! Everyone is waiting for "Someone" else.

The Someone Syndrome creates a fuzziness around decision-making processes. If a client says "Someone" I get right to the point and ask who specifically said it. When we get to the specifics of this "Someone" they often see "Someone" as the impostor it almost always is. This impostor gets in the way of success and spreads fear and doubt. It gets people to abdicate from responsibility. It must be rooted out.

Which Of Your Goals Do You Want Most?

Having rooted out 'someone' it's possible to move forward with what you want to achieve, and since it's usually a few different things you need to decide on the priority. Here's a good story about using my second question.

A man called Peter came to see me and he wanted three things in his life, a Ferrari, a million pounds and to appear on TV. I asked him if that was all he wanted and he said yes. I asked him which he would want to have the most right now out of those three. That is one of the normal questions I would always ask, "Which of your goals do you want most?" I just clear away the clutter. He told me it was the car. I said "fine" and did some hypnosis with him.

About three months later we received a call in the office and it was Peter. He was very excited and said "Gary I've got the car!" I congratulated him. I wasn't sure if he'd robbed a bank to get the money but he'd got his car and I knew it because when he drew up for his second session he could not get it up the ramp! He said happily "Gary, that hypnosis really works. The challenge now is that I am about to sell my business which will realise my one million pounds. Thank you very much. I've also got a chance to appear on TV."

That was interesting. He had wanted all of those things and we had worked on just one.

Can you see the benefit of getting one goal? How it can lead to the others? He could and all I had to do was to get him focused on his TV appearance. From what I gather he did a good job on TV too.

I probably asked him if there was anything else that he might like. That is a typical closing question most sales people would ask. What I wouldn't have done would be to introduce any of my ideas. I wouldn't want to have diluted his 'wanton desires' or to have introduced my thoughts.

I'd be using "Clean Language" on purpose, leaving him free to describe things in his own way. See Wendy Sullivan's chapter later in the book for more on "Clean Language".

If he then came up with something like, "I'd like to be an ambassador for world peace." I'd say "Great, and in addition to that?" My key is to exhaust someone's list to the limits of whatever it is that they want. If it's just one thing then it's just one thing. If it is fifty then it's fifty. Then I ask the same question, "Out of those, which is the one you'd want to have most now?" Then we'd work with that one because that's the king or the queen, that's the orgasmic one. That's the one that makes their toes go "ooh that's good!"

On A Scale Of One To A Hundred, Where Is This Goal On Your 'Wanton Desire Scale'?

I'll ask people "Can you remember when you passed your driving test?" If so I ask, "Did you write that down as a specific goal? Did you go through all the SMART goal setting?" Normally they smile and say, "No, of course not Gary. Don't be stupid." I'll then say "Well, you didn't write it down or go through the specifics. You didn't have a measurement but I'm sure it was in the back of your mind if it wasn't in the forefront." And I'll go on to say: "What I think was in the forefront was wanting to pass your driving test." Normally there will be a particular reason. I'll ask "What was that one reason you wanted to pass your driving test?" And whatever answer they give is obviously their reason.

With some people it's independence. Some people always wanted to drive a car. That one reason was possibly the burning fire within that shone on them every day when they had their driving lessons. That's why they wanted to drive. I say, "Okay then, that would be a one hundred on the Wanton Desire Scale. Does that make sense?" When they say "yes" I invite them to talk about something they want to do now and ask: "On a scale of zero up to one hundred, where one hundred was passing your driving test, where is the thing you want to do now on your Wanton Desire Scale?"

If it's eighty or above there's a good chance they'll get it. If it's seventy five or below they are going to have some struggles because they are not truly committed. Whether they visualise it or feel it, people begin to understand that it's a useful tool. Loads of people say they have used that one with themselves and with family members. It's another great coaching question.

If you are going into a high-powered sales meeting you can use this thinking too. If you can't ask the question just imagine from their responses whether someone is at a "hundred" or "fifty". If they use words like "that sounds interesting" that's fifty or sixty. If they say, "Yes, I could possibly see us being able to use that idea" that would get them up to eighty and if they say, "Absolutely, definitely. When can we bring you in?", that's one hundred and bingo! You can do the deal.

So there you go, those are some of the questions and techniques I use. A taste of the Gary Outrageous approach.

About the Author

Gary Outrageous, the UK's leading Business Hypnotist, loves to share his simple philosophies for health, wealth and happiness. An active hypnotherapist for 17 years, he has helped many people to succeed, from professional footballers to rock stars!

Holder of two world Judo records, Gary knows what is involved in achieving goals and helps people to understand his philosophies in a relaxed yet informative way. He fully understands how to tap into peak performance and how to transfer that skill to others.

Gary runs regular 'GONG' meetings where people hear how to be more successful in life and business from the best speakers in the country.

His keynote presentation "How to use Wanton Desire To Be the BEST!" is filled with solid principles and outrageous philosophies showing you and your teams how to achieve success, incredible wealth and total happiness, personally and professionally.

His speeches are full of "How To's You Can Use", hilarious stories and practical information. They are highly entertaining and teach valuable tools for more successful living. People leave feeling inspired and energised to achieve what they want to be, do or have.

Here are some rave reviews about Gary:

- "The marketing strategy you helped us with was fantastic. Now we have direction, drive and clear goals." Tim Kenyon – Brian Wright(Management Service) Ltd

- "I GOT IT!! I got the £1,000,000 order! All I can say is a massive thank you!" Nigel Robbins FNL

- "The staff have become more customer focused. The sometimes subtle changes you suggested seemed to have a marked effect." Tom Jackson McOpton-partner-Oakwood Eyecare Centre.

For personal development, leadership, sales, customer service, team building or change, Gary's light hearted and memorable ways might just be what you and your organisation need!

To find out more about Gary go to: www.GaryOutrageous.com

Judy Barber

WHAT DO YOU WANT?

BY JULIE FRENCH

Many years ago when I was first dipping my toe into the magical world of NLP (Neuro Linguistic Programming) and was beginning to uncover the workings of the human being, I discovered *the* coaching question... the one question that hits the spot every time. It creates new thoughts, new possibilities, new neurological pathways, new feelings and new ways of being.

And this question is simply...

"What do you want?"

It is such a simple, basic question and yet, having coached hundreds of people over many years, I have found that although it is the question that can produce the most magic, it is also the question that the majority of people find the most difficult to answer.

Just try this as an experiment. Over the next week ask as many people as you can what they want in life, in their work, in their business, or in their most important relationships. Count the number of people whose answers contain either, "I don't know" or "What I don't want is..."

Unfortunately people often know more about what they *don't* want than what they *do* want!

"What's wrong with that?" I hear you ask. Everything! NLP helped me to understand that whatever you focus on in life you tend to attract like a magnet. So if you focus on what you *don't* want then that is precisely what you could end up with.

When I was learning to ski I discovered this by accident... literally. I realised that my body (in this case specifically my legs) took instructions from my conscious mind and my focus. One day, very early on in my skiing career, I nervously spotted what I perceived to be a sheer drop to the side of the beginners' slope. I immediately thought to myself: "Oh no, I don't want to go near that!" Guess where I ended up... Yes! In a very undignified heap in the exact spot that I

Judy Barber

was trying to avoid! I found myself magnetically drawn to the very place I was trying to avoid because that was what I was focusing on.

The human brain is a magnificent organ but you do need to know how it works in order to get the most out of it. One of the things it is helpful to understand is that the brain cannot directly process a negative. For example, if we were walking along together and I said to you: "*Don't* think about tripping over.", what would immediately come to your mind? You would very probably begin to have some kind of thought about tripping over. It might be a picture. It might be a sound. It might be a sensation. It could be all three together! You would have to think about tripping over before you could think about what not tripping over was. Worse still, you would be giving your whole system a command to trip over – not something you want at all! However if I said to you: "*Do* think about walking safely.", your thoughts and your subsequent actions would be more vertical. Much more helpful when you want to stay upright.

You can see that helping people to know what they *do* want can be very useful.

When you know what you want you have something to aim for. You know whether you are on course. You know when you are getting nearer or further away. You know when you are there!

So if it's that simple, why do some people struggle with it and what can you do to help them?

Two good questions to ask anyone who doesn't know what they want are:

"What prevents you from knowing?"

"What would need to happen for you to know?"

What kinds of things can get in the way of people knowing what they want? Some people are afraid to settle on something, to have a particular vision, because they assume that they only get one opportunity to decide what to aim for. They are the kind of people who are afraid of getting it wrong or making a mistake. They need to be reminded that there are no wrong answers and that it's okay to change your mind. If what you first think you want turns out not to be what you wanted, then you can make a new decision and go for something else.

Some people are afraid that if they decide what they want they will have to take some action! They know that could mean stepping over

64

the boundary of their own comfort zone and just the thought of that is enough to create inertia. They need support and encouragement to take some risks. Tony Robbins, the American personal development trainer and author, made the statement: "The level of success you achieve is directly related to the level of uncertainty you can handle." As you step out of your comfort zone, it will expand.

Some people can't get excited about any of the things they are allowing themselves to want because they are thinking too small. The things they are imagining are easily possible for them and as a result are simply uninspiring. They are afraid, or don't feel worthy enough, to go for something more exciting. They need encouragement to think bigger for themselves.

How can you help someone to create a vision that is compelling? A vision that will propel him or her forwards? A vision with a purpose?

You Shall Go To The Ball!

Sometimes when someone is really stuck, I use the 'fairy godmother' model to open things up. It goes something like this:

Just supposing that a fairy godmother (Me for example) knocked on your front door, complete with magic wand, tiara and fairy godmother frock, and made you this offer:

"This is your lucky day. The fairy godmother is in town. Today is the day that you decide to change your life! I have here a magic wand and with it I am able to grant you one thing that you really want. Whatever you want will be yours. You just have to describe specifically what you want. You have five minutes to decide. If you don't want it, I'm off down the road to the house at the end to offer it to someone who *does* know what they want."

Under this kind of pressure, it's amazing how focused many people become.

What kind of requests do people tend to make and how can you help them to approach their answer in the most effective way for them? Robert Dilts, the prolific author and NLP trainer, developed a wonderful model, which helps us to understand how people are thinking. It is based on the idea that there are different ways of approaching any kind of problem, including learning and change. It is called the "Neurological Levels" model.

Neurological Levels

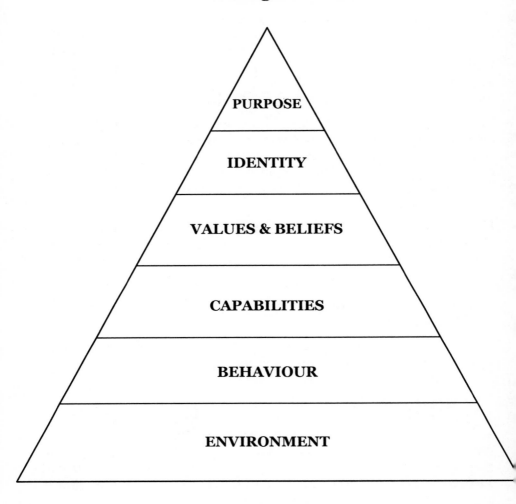

At the most basic level there is the **environment**. "How satisfied are you with your environment?", "How do you want it to be different?", "What 'things' do you want?" etc.

Often at this level people focus on money, houses, cars and other material things. Very often when people set goals for themselves they tend to want to acquire material wealth.

The next level is related to **behaviour**. "What are you doing now?", "What actions are you taking?", "What are you not doing that you would like to be doing?", "What would you like to do differently?" etc.

These kinds of wants would be things like going round the world, losing weight, stopping smoking or stopping procrastinating.

The next level is about your **skills and capabilities**. "What skills do you currently have and what skills would you like to acquire?", "Is there something that you would like to learn to do?" etc. Examples would include things like learning to play golf or learning a new language.

The next level relates to your **values and beliefs**. "What is important to you now and how well is this reflected in the way you live your life?" , "Are you living according to your true values?" , "What are your beliefs about life, about yourself and about how possible it is for things to be different?" etc. This could include things like achieving more balance in your life and prioritising your family, your business or yourself. It could involve developing new beliefs about life, other people or yourself.

The next level is about your sense of who you are and of your **identity**. "How comfortable are you with your self and who you are?", "Who are you?", "Who do you want to become more like?" and most important of all, "What is your purpose?", "Why are you here?", "What is the meaning of your life?"

Work From The Top Down Not The Bottom Up

Material things can be very seductive. Many people want more things. Sometimes despite focusing on and acquiring a lot of things, a person still doesn't have a sense of personal fulfilment, inner peace or contentment. The levels are not aligned. When you have clarity at the highest level about why you are here, the answer to the question: "What do you want?" becomes so much more straightforward to answer on all the levels below. Everything falls into place because you have alignment from the top down.

How Can People Know What They Want?

When you are helping someone to know what they want, questions from you relating to the higher levels will help them to answer questions at the lower levels. This ensures they have alignment and therefore ensures they can sustain any changes that they make. When you have reached this point you know your whole being is in tune with your decision at all levels.

Unconscious Wisdom

Once you know what you want, the next thing is to imprint your unconscious mind with the right messages to ensure continued success.

One Sunday morning before going out for a run I was relaxing and reading a book called, "Blink, The Power of Thinking Without Thinking" by Malcolm Gladwell. I came across something that could potentially have adversely affected my ability to run well that morning. It was about a word scramble test which had words such as 'worried', 'old', 'lonely' and 'wrinkle' concealed within it. The words were not picked up consciously because the conscious part of the mind was busy solving the puzzle of how to make a sentence of the words.

These 'hidden' words actually had the effect of slowing down the students undertaking the test. The research showed that people doing the test including the negative words moved more slowly when leaving the room in which the test had taken place than those who were exposed to other more energetic words.

As I was reading the book and doing the test myself I began to notice a sluggish feeling in my body – not good preparation for a run! I decided I needed to take immediate action to change this feeling and I started to experiment with writing and gazing at other more energising words on a page. As I did so I noticed a good response in my body, a more energetic feeling, so I wrote some more words. This time I wrote them on a brightly-coloured card. I wrote the word 'RUN' in the centre of the card and added words around it such as 'energy', 'fun' , 'easy', 'light' , 'movement' and 'flow'. I gazed at the card before setting off for my run and I felt a wonderful feeling of energy and lightness as I ran.

When I returned home, refreshed and inspired, I started to experiment with writing down other words and other concepts using coloured cards. I started to put my goals in the centre and to put other words around them that would give me a positive focus and a great feeling. I find this is even more effective when you distract your conscious mind by giving it a task to do while you are gazing at the card. It could be something like singing a song, reciting something backwards or even doing a puzzle.

So when you help yourself or others to align their neurological levels by asking, "What do you want?" and using positive language you can be just as helpful as a fairy godmother!

About the Author

When I was 10, I spent almost the whole of one summer holiday standing on the top diving board of our local swimming pool, desperately wanting to have the courage to jump off. Each day I would say to myself and to my friends "today is the day". I would make my way to the top and stand, looking down at the water far below me, and I would wait and wait. I would wait for the right time. Of course there wasn't one!

As an adult, it was a pattern that I became familiar with. Fear would hold me back and even though I did eventually jump many times, there were times when I didn't and there were many times when I spent longer than I needed to spend looking down at the water.

In November 2002, I left my full time job as a senior manager in Social Services with 25 years of local government employment under my belt, and I jumped! It was one of the best decisions of my life. I am now a co-director of the Academy of High Achievers, a company that runs achievement programmes for success orientated people who want to continue to grow. Our programmes include residential NLP Practitioner training and Executive coaching programmes. Check out our website at www.aha-success.com

Judy Barber

PART THREE: USING COACHING QUESTIONS IN THE WORLD AT LARGE

These chapters, by their variety, show the wide scope of practical applications there are for coaching and coaching questions. Richard Tod uses coaching questions in working with local government. Tessa Lovemore uses specific coaching questions for different groups of people when working with bullying situations. George Metcalfe uses coaching questions in networking. Martin Haworth uses a different question with each of three coaching clients. Steve Halls uses questions in fitness coaching and Gérard Jakimavicius uses coaching questions in business development.

What different situations are you aware of in your life where using coaching questions could be beneficial?

Judy Barber

WHY ARE YOU HERE AND WHAT ARE YOU DOING?

BY RICHARD TOD

COMBINING SKILLS AND EXPERIENCE

The next time you are at a party, take time to wander round and find out a bit about the people in the room. Note their background, skills, experience and knowledge. Now, how it would be if all of those people had to work together to resolve an issue in your locality? How powerful would their combined knowledge be in finding a solution? Despite any rumours to the contrary, people in my field, which is local government, are not much different from anyone else –like the people you met at that party.

Local politicians have a strong need to "do something" about the world. Whether you agree with precisely what each "something" is you can respect their ability to get out of the house and become involved. Do you and others you know also have a strong need to 'do something', for example about your organisation or the environment?

If the experience and skills of a group of people are combined then the potential for problem resolution and creativity is huge. In my experience with local government that potential is not always realised.

PROBLEMS

When voted into office councillors meet political, bureaucratic, financial, legal, media and community blockages to what they want to do. This is where problems start. Councillors may soon learn that doing nothing is far easier than running the gauntlet of change where it seems everyone wants to block, berate, ridicule and harass.

There are successful councillors who take risks and face bad press with enthusiasm, but it takes a strong character to fight against daily criticism and negativity. We cannot be surprised that many prefer to withdraw into their shells, becoming less than effective in leading the community so that a downward spiral of community perception gathers momentum. Then fewer people bother to vote and they are more prepared to believe media criticism without question.

I'll give you an example:

The media loved it when our council made a decision to improve facilities for kids because they said the council had ignored the community around the new facility who don't want all the kids around. However, if the kids wander around without facilities the media will attack the councillors for not looking after young people! "Of course the press are speaking in the public interest!"

Only the strong can maintain any enthusiasm against this kind of negativity. For the rest, it is usually a case of either finding a niche committee or group where they can feel of some use or directing their frustrations into political in-fighting.

Some resign themselves to dealing with issues like street lighting and dog muck, passing on complaints from the community and passing back responses from officers with no real involvement. Often their frustration spills out onto attacking council officers for things like failing to repair a street sign or being slow to implement a manifesto. Long serving councillors can become sceptical, slow to change and overly cautious.

The problems here are:
- Obstacles and blockages sapping the strength from intention and motivation.
- Withdrawal into a protective comfort zone that prevents effective leadership.
- Venting frustration through internal politics.
- scepticism, conservatism and risk-aversion.

Does any of this describe you or people in your organisation? Can you identify similar problems in yourself or people you work with? Perhaps they stem from being unable to keep up motivation in the face of apparently insurmountable blocks or from painful criticism.

NEW WAYS OF WORKING

My current role is to interest local councillors in and involve them with new ways of working. I use the questions "Why are you here?" to help people reconnect to what motivates them, and "What are you doing?" to encourage action.

WHY ARE YOU HERE?

The secret to reviving enthusiasm is taking people back to the reason they took on a role in the first place. "Why are you here?" reminds them of the passion they once felt.

With a councillor it might be the feeling of success they felt when their votes were counted. This is not that tough as the adrenalin rush from a successful political campaign and victory after an interminably long counting of votes is not easily forgotten.

Perhaps that's similar to the excitement of deciding to set up a new business or being the successful applicant for a job. When have you felt passionate about a new role or project?

Even if most of the experiences with that role or project have been negative there will have been some experiences of success - and the odd positive experience will be unforgettable! Remembering the positive is essential for reawakening passion. For someone it might just be passion for not changing and for staying with the status quo. Even this can be a positive starting point because initially it's just reawakening some passion that is important. The state to enable is one in which people feel good about themselves, a state which is then reinforced and anchored in their minds.

Once that state is established criticism and bad press can be seen for what they are relative to the hopes and aspirations someone has for themselves and their community. My way of overcoming the negatives has always been to remind myself that, "If I'm getting loads of bad press then at least I'm doing something in the community. The critics, generally, are not."

The learning points here are:

- Remember your passion.
- Remember times when you have been successful.
- Remember the feelings of passion and success.
- Build self-esteem.
- From feeling good about yourself, get the negatives into perspective.

WHAT ARE YOU DOING?

When someone is firmly in a state of self congratulation the next step is to ask: "What are you doing?" Reflecting on the person they have become relative to the person they had aspired to be brings realism about their current state and brings with it a desire to change.

It is necessary to underpin remembered passion by confronting each blockage or obstacle and I use questions like these:

- What can you tell me about this obstacle?
- How can you discover whether it is of your own making?
- Can it be changed in some way?
- If it isn't of your making, can you change your approach and turn it to your advantage?
- Can you use ingenuity to find an alternative route around it?

The learning points here are to:

- Bring realism by comparing past aspiration with current behaviour.
- Build interest in moving from current behaviour to aspiration.
- Work with each obstacle to progress in turn.

At a Welsh County Council, after an introductory presentation in which I presented these thoughts, I was approached by a large, dignified, elderly councillor well into his 70s. His massive frame was only slightly stooped and his handshake shook my whole arm as he beamed and boomed a Welsh thank you. He told me that he had not been so roused since hearing a speech by the eminent Welsh Politician Aneurin Bevan back in 1952. I hardly think my presentation was comparable! It was not the presentation but his realisation that he could still achieve things that made him so enthusiastic. This gentleman subsequently became part of a group of highly motivated councillors who made a surprise coup and took over the leadership of the council. The Leadership had not attended the sessions and were perhaps not capable of dealing with the new found enthusiasm for change.

CREATING CHANGE

The acceptance and defence of: 'What is and has always been is the only way to do it.' must be the greatest blockage to progress in any aspect of life, and it certainly can be in government! You've heard the quote: "If it isn't broken don't fix it.", but my favoured quote is from Charles Kettering, Inventor and Pioneer: "If you have always done it that way then you are probably doing it wrong."

The process of knocking down blockages can be fraught when people seek to defend the indefensible and bad habits sometimes die hard. However, bringing back good memories can give people space to think about knocking down what they don't really want to defend.

Using positive language, having people feel they can ask questions and achieving critical mass are also important.

POSITIVE LANGUAGE

Here's an example of unhelpful language in government. Councillors not in the Executive are called 'Back Bench' members. The term implies that they are reserves who are pulled off the benches once in a while to vote and put back again when not required. I encourage councillors to see their role in more positive terms, such as 'Front

Line Councillors' leading their communities, developing policies and helping the executive drive the council forward.

Are there any traditional terms used in your organisation that are perpetuating negative perceptions and attitudes?

There are certain key words that I find turn councillors off almost immediately. One example is 'training'. If you want that critical mass to attend your training session you better call it a 'seminar' or a 'debate'!

Another example is 'customer focussed methodology' How many people are motivated by that? How about using 'customer friendly' instead? It is worth spending time researching what terms switch people off in your organisation.

ASKING QUESTIONS

In my experience, in small groups, inhibitions are reduced and people feel free to ask questions that they might have felt were stupid in a larger group. A question might be "Why do we do such and such?" Admitting you don't know something is easier in a small group. Often the answer is "We don't know either." These kinds of superficially 'stupid' questions are not stupid at all and help break down the barriers to working relationships. They enable people to see issues from different perspectives and to set free the creativity essential to move forward.

CRITICAL MASS

In any organisation the voices of just one or two motivated people can soon be lost in a crowd of negatives. If my work with councillors is to have any chance of a lasting impact then I must motivate a 'critical mass' of councillors so that they are able to see the process of change through to completion in spite of all the obstacles to change in a bureaucratic organisation.

Knowing where they are today with a vision of where they want to be in the future is more than half the 'battle'. To ensure that the 'battle' is eventually won the motivation of sufficient people is essential and it needs to be constantly reinforced by the leadership. There is no point in employing consultants and trainers if the lessons learnt are not taken forward. The leadership must ensure that enough people have been involved in the training and that they are supported in implementing recommendations for change.

> I worked with others coaching in a London Borough Council and we managed to get a good percentage of the councillors to our sessions including some of the Leadership. At the time the effect on individual councillors seemed varied and we were not confident that we had achieved sufficient numbers of supporters. We need not have worried. It soon became clear that the process we had started continued after we were gone and those who still had some doubts were persuaded by their colleagues. We had achieved sufficient momentum for the enthusiasm for change to be self-sustaining.

HOPE FOR THE FUTURE

Councillors give up a large part of their lives for no real financial gain, receive constant criticism and, frequently, public contempt. They are individuals with a common attribute:

They are committed to 'doing'
something for their communities.

In my job I hope that by changing the way in which they work councillors will actually be able to do, and be seen to be doing, more for their communities. They may then receive less criticism and encourage the community to become more engaged in the democratic process - which will benefit us all!

Imagine how that kind of change could enable you to achieve what you want to do for others and affect **your** business or work!

I find combining the questions "Why are you here?" and "What are you doing?" with consideration of the blocks to progress is the best way to enable change. I hope they are helpful to you as coaching questions for yourself and for working with others to renew motivation whether it's in government, business, the public sector or a voluntary organisation.

Happily councillors are not alone in wanting to 'do something' to help others. The potential for 'doing something' is only limited by perceived blocks to action. What possibilities are there when you consider combining the human need to take action with the creative capacity of groups of people? I believe there's hope for the future in the answers to that question.

About the Author

Richard Tod is a freelance consultant working in local government who specialises in helping elected members to understand their responsibilities and to know how to use their powers.

His background as a Leader of a Borough Council combined with his years as a consultant in the private sector have provided Richard with a unique and detached view of local government and the people in it.

Richard has worked on contracts on behalf of the Improvement development Agency, the Welsh Local Government Association and SOLACE Enterprises (The commercial wing of the Society of Local Government Chief Executives and Senior Officers) and is an Associate of the Association for Public Sector Excellence (APSE).

Richard is contracted to a number of authorities, from Districts to London Borough and County Councils. These projects are all variations on a theme for training councillors that Richard devised for SOLACE Enterprises.

As a Council Leader, Richard was involved in significant organisational change both at administrative and political levels. The huge programme of change was set in a background of low staff morale and serious financial problems. Within only 3 years the authority was able to reverse its fortunes, effect real improvements in the local economic climate and significantly improve staff morale.

Richard spent over 20 years as a consultant and senior manager mainly involved in designing and implementing organisational and operational change. His projects vary from the manufacture of plastic buckets to installing machines for growing grass at the edge of the Borneo jungle and contract management of large construction projects in the London Docklands.

He is now studying to qualify as a Life Coach and says it is about time he qualified in what he has been doing most of his working life.

Contact Richard at Richardtod@onetel.com

ARE YOU WILLING TO SAVE YOUR SELF ESTEEM?

BY TESSA LOVEMORE

In my experience, everyone is vulnerable to bullying in the same way that anyone will eventually succumb to torture. It may be that some people are more vulnerable than others, but the most common mistake is to assume that victims of bullying do something to bring it on themselves. The simple facts are that bullying is a powerful way of controlling the emotional response of another and that bullies are themselves insecure.

All too often victims are described as having something different about them that exposes them to bullying. Yet, we are all different in some way: so it can't be difference that causes bullying. However, it is true that bullies focus on difference. In extreme historical cases this bullying has led to the holocaust, ethnic or race debasement, and religious hatred. It is clear that focusing on difference leads to devastating consequences: and it emphasises how important it is in fields of coaching, counselling, business and education to recognise that victims are not bound to be victims because they are different.

However, where victims are different is that they are: children or adults, boys or girls, men or women. Understanding these differences is helpful in knowing what questions we need to ask. Thus, in this chapter I will begin with what happens for all those affected by bullying, and then focus on what questions help different ages and genders who suffer from bullying.

Bullying Is A Self-Esteem Issue

Both bullies and victims are at risk. Victims lose self-esteem, become depressed, nervous, fearful and ill: while bullies isolate themselves from genuine relationships. For, while bullies may think they are supported by those who don't challenge their bullying behaviour, their support comes from those who are only too glad that they themselves have not been singled out. In this way bullies get themselves into a tight corner, as they need to remain vicious to maintain their support: and the more vicious they get the more their relationships are based on fear. For this reason I believe that bullying can cause immeasurable psychological and social damage both to the victim and the bully. In some cases when bullying is institutional, or presents a danger, the wisest action may be to move away from the situation.

However, as both bullies and victims experience low self-esteem and confidence, the questions we need to ask bullies and victims should focus on improving their self-esteem.

Lipstick, Dust, Cakes And Self-Esteem

Shavelson with other researchers has conducted almost 30 years of research on what we think about ourselves and how it affects our confidence, in other words on how we perceive our value and competence. Their research shows how self-esteem is structured from our every-day life experiences. For example, the more often we experience the same outcome from what we do (or what is done to us) the more fixed that perception of our ability becomes.

Put simply, when we do something we perceive as easy, we feel fine about repeating it at any time. On the other hand, if we do something that does not work out very well it unnerves us to the point that we may avoid it the next time. Similarly, if someone responds negatively to something specific that we do or say, we begin to lose confidence in that area. However, the most noteworthy result of Shavelson's research is the discovery that if we continue to experience negativity in one area, it starts to undermine our confidence in *all* areas.

For example, I am not generally afraid of home-making skills and I know that I make even the most humble home look pleasant. In fact, there is no use beating around the bush: I am a good cook and I have a talent for making my home look lovely. Yet, when my mother-in-law used to visit, my cakes flopped and the most grotesque dust balls would materialise from under the furniture. Funnily, the more she made it known publicly that I was not good enough, the more my cakes failed to rise and my fear of dust intensified. So, to this day I avoid making cakes and even the slightest disorder in my home makes me feel slovenly.

Another example: When my mother asks me if I am ill, it is usually that I am not wearing lipstick. If I am wearing lipstick, she tells me how nice I look. So, if you see me wearing lipstick it means I am not feeling confident.

It may seem that I am treating this fairly lightly – talking about lipstick, dust and cakes – but it illustrates that my self-esteem is fragile in areas such as appearance, dust and baking. Yet, my own experiences show me that when someone says they are not good at something, it probably means they have experienced negative responses rather than that they are truly lacking skills. Statements like these reveal much about our self-esteem, and ultimately self-confidence. In fact, anything and everything we do, or the things that are said to us and done to us, help to form our self-esteem.

Low self-esteem paralyses, creates feelings of helplessness and inhibits learning and coping strategies. Yet improving self-esteem may be complicated because people lose self-esteem in tacit or subtle ways. Also the ways children and adults, or males and females, lose self-esteem seem to be different. For this reason we need to take into account who we are helping and what affects their self-esteem. When we come to coaching people to cope with bullying, and its effects, our approach must take into account age *and* gender.

Coaching Children

Research shows that young children rapidly lose self-esteem across a wide range of abilities when they experience negativity regarding *any* aspect of themselves. Also, young children are less able to distinguish between specific abilities and aspects of themselves. So that experiencing negativity about something specific like drawing can lower their confidence as a person in general. This means that even in our efforts to help children improve their abilities – by offering advice on how they could do better – we could be lowering their confidence and ultimately their self-esteem.

So, the rule I follow is to help to value the child for who and what they are, and to help those around them to do the same. My questions then are focused on what they do, what they like to do and what makes them happy. When the focus is on developing an appreciation of the uniqueness of the child then the child experiences a real value in themselves. So, when I ask a child questions, I try to develop a genuine interest in their perspective of what they enjoy doing. In the same way, when I question the adults involved with a child, my genuine interest in their child helps them to see unique aspects of their child too.

Ultimately, feeling valued boosts confidence and self-esteem. The most common mistakes we make with children's self-esteem issues (and, in this case, if they are being bullied) is to offer advice or training in how to cope with bullies. Simply assuming that they cannot cope without our practical advice may subtly undermine their confidence. This is so difficult for parents and carers who have experienced bullying themselves, as they know how frightening it feels to be bullied. However, the best protection against bullying is to feel worthy, valued and able.

Furthermore, from Maslow, psychology has learned that children need to feel healthy, safe and loved to have positive self-esteem. Maslow's work has also shown that everyone needs to have positive self-esteem to be able to learn. That is why I cannot emphasise the following enough: **The job of protecting children from bullying, or danger of any kind, is ours - as adults, and not the child's: and teaching children to protect themselves is not only counter-productive but it doesn't work.**

Coaching Teenagers

Teenagers also need to feel valued. But most importantly, they need to feel that what they *think* is valued. For this reason, my advice to all people involved with teenagers is – *get stupid*. In other words: the more we show that we know more, can offer good advice, or ask probing questions the more we lower their trust in themselves. In fact, we help the most when we develop a genuine interest in what they think. More importantly, develop an interest in what they find interesting, and most importantly not in what *you* find interesting!

So, when helping teenagers, I try to stifle my impulse to add what I have experienced (and what I know) to allow them to trust me with their thoughts. This means that my questions are less planned and more genuine, with the result that my genuine interest communicates my genuine value of their thoughts.

Ultimately, the questions we need to ask teenagers suffering from bullying are inner questions. They may be questions we never voice, but simply communicate by genuine interest. Try it – it works!

Coaching Men And Women

We still have much to learn about the self-esteem of men and women. Social research tends to argue that many differences are due to conditioning. Popular psychology claims men and women are different when it comes to interests and relationships. Medical science also points out differences in the ways the sexes function and think. Yet, in coaching and counselling we need to consider both positions, the commonalities and the differences. For example, the self-esteem of men and women may be threatened in the same way in the workplace because the focus is on effectiveness. In areas of personal fulfilment and relationships their self-esteem suffers differently.

Clearly, women in general construct much of their positive self-esteem on a wide range of factors such as relationships and homemaking skills while men seem more prone to lose self-esteem when their aspirations are thwarted, their actions lead nowhere and their achievements are not valued.

However, many women lose self-esteem if they are denied recognition for characteristically male factors: and men lose self-esteem if only valued for their deeds. These characteristic gender factors become a double-edged sword because experiencing failure in any area of life erodes self-esteem. Thus, our questions to men or women need to focus on improving self-esteem in areas attributed to both genders.

Unlike children and teenagers, adults respond well to learning how their self-esteem is constructed. You can use questions like: "What made you decide you could not do something?" and "What event started you feeling this way about yourself?" To demonstrate how self-esteem is caused by positive or negative experiences I would follow up questions like these with something like: "What experience of success (no matter how small) have you had in the same area?" or, "Given the opportunity to succeed, how would you prepare yourself to try it again?"

Thus, our questions should help clients see that their self-esteem can change by:

- challenging their perceptions of failure,
- valuing their individuality, and
- setting themselves up to succeed.

Finally, clients need to know that some bullying can be resolved by confronting the bully but that most bullies have low self-esteem and therefore will react adversely to any criticism. Therefore, in the long run, using some of the techniques I have described in this chapter to promote positive self-esteem in the bully may be the answer.

Self-esteem based on appearance is particularly precarious and perhaps best left aside as a specific topic in favour of building general self-esteem. Improved self-esteem changes the way we appear to others and has long lasting value in maintaining continued positive self-esteem.

In this chapter I have showed that asking questions to improve self-esteem is an efficient way of dealing with bullying. It is about reconstructing a genuine appreciation of self. Victims of bullying need to truly value themselves in order to be able to respond positively in difficult relationships. We need to ask the definitive question: "Are you willing to save your self-esteem?"

About the Author

Tessa Lovemore loves walking in the countryside, swimming in the sea, having fun, beautifying ugly spaces and socialising. She is an experienced:

- Wife
- Mother (natural and foster)
- Counsellor
- Teacher
- Teacher Trainer
- Education Consultant
- Specialist in behaviour and learning

Tessa is passionate about improving the quality of lives and is skilled in dealing with difficult situations in relationships and education matters. She offers unique insights into the deeper aspects of human relationships and development. She also has a way of bringing these insights into every day language and experience.

Before venturing into social science Tessa worked as a schoolteacher in Britain and overseas for approximately twenty years. She now divides her time between research, counselling, advising in schools, lecturing and running courses. Her counselling is based on the work of Carl Rogers and insights from Anthroposophy and she teaches a range of subjects relating to children's learning.

Out of her own research she has developed courses on the ways children develop emotionally and socially, the development of love in relationships, and historical changes in soul development. She runs courses in Britain and abroad on:

- Love and ways of developing love in relationships
- How children learn from play and stories
- Sensory development in children
- Keys to understanding the ways children think and behave

Tessa has published work in the fields of the effects of television, children's behaviour, and counselling. She is currently writing up six years of research into teachers' understanding of children's moral development. Tessa has ambitions to see more of the world, enjoy writing helpful books, have lots more fun, and most importantly find ways to improve the lives of street children in South Africa.

You can contact Tessa by e-mail: tessa.lovemore@gmail.com

Judy Barber

WHO DO YOU KNOW WHO...?

BY GEORGE METCALFE

I invented the term "Fearless Networking" when I was training Barclays Bank relationship managers and quickly realised they hated networking. Many of them retain the old idea of us customers going to them on bended knees hoping they will give us an overdraft or other financial help. But the new bank manager must go out into the marketplace to solicit business in a highly competitive age.

I figured if I could find some way of making networking fun, they would become Fearless Networkers.

"Networking is the cultivating of mutually beneficial, give-and-take, win-win relationships," says Bob Burg, doyen of American networkers. I have his personal permission to incorporate many of his brilliant networking ideas and pieces of advice in this chapter. His book 'Endless Referrals' published by McGraw-Hill (ISBN 0-07-008997-3) is my networking bible and has been a prime influence in my networking success.

The Oxford Dictionary description of networking serves our purposes beautifully: "A group of people who exchange information, contact, and experience for professional or social purposes."

Did you know referrals generate 80% more results than cold calls? Approximately 70% of jobs are found through Networking. It is exciting to know that anyone you might want to meet or contact is only four to five people away from you. You only have to do a little research and ask the magic question, "Who do you know who...?"

Fearless Networking is a way of life for many successful people. It can be your moral support and backup system when building new friendships, moving jobs or moving cities. It is extremely valuable in starting or expanding your business. Who has never asked their own network of friends for recommendations for a builder, plumber, or electrician? Among the best networkers are mothers with small children.

My best networking result was totally unexpected. I met a potential client at a networking meeting. We worked together and became great friends. He introduced me to his friends. We share an interest in motorbiking. To my absolute amazement, last year they presented me with the fabulous Yamaha FJR 1300 motorcycle you see me riding in my photograph.

According to experts who teach marketing to coaches there are two important ways of getting new business, networking actively and obtaining opportunities for public speaking.

In my networking seminars I often start by asking: "What is it that we might fear or dislike most about networking?" Here are some fears which come up regularly:

- Rejection
- I might be boring
- Getting stuck with somebody I don't like
- Being an insensitive salesperson
- I don't know enough and might be "found out" as phoney
- They may not like me.
- I might not follow up.
- I will be forgotten.
- I am shy with strangers.
- I may not be accepted.
- They are more important than me

Just as we are at the centre of our own network, everybody else is at the centre of *their* network, which is as it should be. Each person in a network is a source of support (referrals, help, information, etc.) for everyone else. This is powerful when we realise that everyone in our network is part of other people's networks. This includes immediate family members, distant relatives, close friends, casual acquaintances, your doctors, postmen, plumbers, tailors and hairdressers – in fact practically anybody who touches your life and whose life you touch.

We each have a personal sphere of influence of about 250 people.

Cultivate your network and your personal sphere of influence will soar to incredible heights. I have a personal database of well over 3,000 names – clearly the result of a gloriously misspent life! At business networking breakfasts when there may be 20 people present,

I like to imagine there are 5000 people filling the room and that each of those people could network for me.

Networking is more than just a good idea. It is an opportunity to develop relationships and create a community. It enhances and enriches lives and is a way of life in itself. It is a tremendously effective way to help you accomplish goals.

Networking Abuses

- Collecting business cards without making personal connections
- Trying to make the sale right there and then
- Focusing on one's own agenda rather than listening with interest
- Intruding inappropriately
- Walking over people and forgetting the value of taking time to develop relationships
- Getting caught up in quantity before quality

Keys To Unlocking Fearless Networking

1) Goodbye Lone Ranger

Underlying our culture is the idea that we are supposed to be superhumans accomplishing major feats alone, never asking for help or showing signs of being in difficulty.

How often have you heard somebody say: "If you want a job done right do it yourself!" This 'Lone Ranger mentality' is a stumbling block for potential networkers.

Try these Fearless Networker thoughts:

- I can do this quickly and easily by working with resources in my network.
- I enjoy others contributing to me and helping me with my goals.
- I willingly learn from others.
- By working with others I learn new and better ways to handle challenges.
- People appreciate opportunities to contribute expertise to me.
- People feel included and appreciated when I approach them for assistance or ideas.
- I am confident about letting others know my needs.

- People think I am resourceful when I ask questions.
- I am enthusiastic about benefiting from the expertise and support of others.

2) Expect Nothing In Return

This means contributing to and supporting others without 'keeping score'. When you trust people, you know they will do their best, reciprocate when they can and serve you as *they* have been served. It may seem scary giving up the scoreboard but you can't use it for control or influence anymore. Take the initiative to give, participate and contribute, and benefits will come back to you, although not necessarily immediately or even from the same person. In fact, often they come back from unexpected places.

3) Face Fears

Fears stop us from making calls, asking for referrals or asking for support. They can be dealt with by questions and listening. Don't let these stop you:

I can't stand rejection! Nobody likes it. Yet if we consider that Networking consists of gathering, collecting and distributing information, then when we contact someone to let them know we are looking for a referral, a prospect or career opportunities, we are giving them information. Our focus is distributing information to a sufficient number of people to make connections that will serve us in getting support, contacts and reaching our goals.

Obligation. Fearless Networking involves giving without expectations or score-keeping and therefore no obligations. When you treat people with respect and give your best, you have done your part.

Looking weak or needy. We must realise that asking for support is not a sign of weakness but of strong self-esteem and a commitment to the goal rather than the ego. It demonstrates willingness and ability to learn from others and shows we are inclusive not exclusive.

Appearing pushy and aggressive. You don't have to be that way to get results, although it is important to participate and interact with people. Networking requires patience and persistence, just like planting seeds.

Being impersonal, forced and cold. Networking only seems impersonal if there is no focus on relationships and the only agenda is getting results. Networking is the genuine expression of interest in others and willingness to contribute and support.

4) Be Interested Vs Interesting

Our greatest assets as coaches are ignorance and hunger for knowledge. These, coupled with the magic attribute of empathy, will protect us virtually from all social harm. So ask lots of open questions and genuinely listen to the answers.

5) Invest In Relationships

Make every effort to be friends with people, noticing their needs and being useful. In the long run this is more important than them doing something for you. People do business with, and refer business to, people they know, like, and trust.

6) Asking Questions

This really is the key that opens the magic box to Fearless Networking. Many coaches know the 'Five Step Coaching Process', a very good method of developing brilliantly confident networking skills. It emphasises using open questions. Most people like being asked questions. They love talking about themselves and/or their businesses.

The Five steps are:

1. **Listen**
   Fearless Networkers encourage talking through listening intently. Initial statements are often not the full truth: that comes later when trust is established. Maintain total eye contact. Don't interrupt. Try listening for three minutes without speaking. It's a long time but just wait for the nuggets to appear! Use silence even with taciturn people. Follow the 80% Listening; 20% Speaking rule. When listening watch for your own internal voice, which can be a terrible distraction. Focus on listening skills and the relationship will build naturally. If you are networking correctly, people will never know!

2. **Evoke**
   Prompt for more information by saying 'uh huh', 'really', 'yes'.

Repeat the last word or idea. Use open questions to bring out someone's own thoughts and ideas.

3. **Clarify**
   Say: "I'm sorry, I didn't understand what you said" to help someone clarify their thinking. Ask about the most important thing someone is saying: "Can you be specific about that?"

4. **Discuss**
   Discussion at the introduction stage must be non-judgemental, unless someone asks your opinion. Even if they do ask your opinion be cautious about offering it.

5. **Support**
   "How can I help?" Is an excellent question to complete the exchange.

Ten Networking Questions That Work Every Time

1. How did you get started in business?

2. What do you enjoy most about your job/profession?

3. What separates you and your company from the competition? (a 'permission to boast' question)

4. What advice would you give someone starting in your business? (lets your new Networking prospect be a mentor)

5. What one thing would you do with your business if you knew you could not fail?

6. What significant changes have you seen in your profession?

7. What are the coming trends in your business?

8. What's the strangest or funniest incident you ever experienced in your business?

9. What have you found to be most effective for promoting your business?

10. What one sentence would you like people to use in describing the way you do business?

It's How You Ask... But note how important the 'What?' word is in eliciting great answers.

Questions should make the other person feel good.

A useful Extender Question... "Really? Tell me more"

The Echo Technique. Just repeat the last few words of the networking prospect's sentence in order to keep him or her talking.

Always have in mind the "Who do you know who...?" question.

One of my best business-building questions is "What's bugging you right now?" It's far more effective than asking somebody what their problems are! As a coach I might later follow up by asking whether it might be helpful if we could together eliminate whatever is causing anxiety or annoyance.

The One Key Question That Separates the Pros From the Amateurs:

"How can I know if someone I am talking to is a good prospect for you?"

How To Work Any Crowd

- Remember names. Develop memory hooks...
- Introduce people to others. (Then you are a 'centre of influence'. Give people warm introductions, showing you are someone who is potentially good to do business with.)
- Adjust your attitude. You are there to work and build your network, but that doesn't mean you can't have fun!
- Work the crowd. Be sincere and have an air of confidence. Smile. Be pleasant and approachable.
- When appropriate act as a 'host' and pass bottles and canapés around.
- Ask people questions about themselves and their business, not yourself and your business.
- Don't forget to ask for your Networking prospect's business card.
- Later on, pop back and call that person by name before you leave.

Useful Follow-up Techniques

- Send personalised thank you notes. I use postcards

- Try to incorporate something like this: "Thank you. It was a pleasure meeting you. If ever I can refer business your way, I certainly will."
- Keep your networking prospects in your thoughts, including sending relevant newspaper articles, clippings and information that might relate to their business.
- Send thank you notes after receiving referrals.

Key Characteristics of Successful Networkers

Positivity

Motivation

Trustworthiness

Listening

Commitment

Curiosity

Asking for help

Sharing successes

Reliability

Courage

Remembering

Patience

My Top Ten Rules For Fearless Networking

Rule 1. Be there.

Rule 2. Be more interested in who you talk to than in yourself.

Rule 3. Be enthusiastic about the other person's ideas and plans.

Rule 4. Make what you do sound exciting and keep it short.

Rule 5. Record details of meetings. Follow up quickly.

Rule 6. Do everything to GIVE, rather than GAIN.

Rule 7. Boldly refer/introduce people to others.

Rule 8. Understand that asking questions makes you interesting.

Rule 9. There's no such thing as selling – only research.

Rule 10. You are terrific – but forget that when talking to others!

Join all the networking groups you have energy for. Weekly breakfast meetings are organised throughout the UK by the Business Referral Exchange (www.brenet.co.uk) and Business Network International (www.bni-europe.com). You can deliver a 60 second speech each time to give and get referrals. Membership over the years has been worth thousands of pounds to me. Join Ecademy (www.ecademy.com), the internet networking organisation with over 50,000 members. Attend Speed Networking events, for example beyourownboss.tiscali.co.uk and www.yesgroup.org. Go to Chambers of Commerce meetings. Join or support charity organisations, (one of mine is the Prince's Trust and I've got paying clients from mentoring there). Get actively involved with a political party.

Networking works for me. Last year I referred over £2,000,000 worth of business to other people, some of which paid me in generous commissions. It can work for you too.

About the Author

The Life & Business Strategy Coach

George Metcalfe is one of the original English life coaches and a founder member of the 800-strong EuroCoach List to which he contributes frequently. He studied under the late, great, Thomas Leonard, founder of Coach University, and has coached hundreds of people privately and corporately over the last decade. He served as a vice president of the UK International Coach Federation.

He continues as a driving force in encouraging coaches to take an active part in networking as a powerful means of building their own businesses and was president of the Business Referral Exchange (BRE) in 2003. A frequent lecturer on networking, during 2004 he referred over £2,000,000 worth of business to other people.

His background of 35 years as chairman of international public relations firms working in over 30 countries and 14 years as principal of a management consultancy provides him with a unique focus on coaching. He has, in essence, been coaching and training all his life – including developing fencing, boxing and pentathlon teams – and working professionally with political and business leaders and members of the public. His prime purpose as a coach is encouraging people to make the absolute best of their potential, becoming fulfilled, productive and profitable.

He has advised governments and major industries. At one time he wrote and presented his own children's TV programme. He has written several books and served on the Westminster City Council and the old Inner London Education Authority. He is a trustee of the Hanover Foundation, which trains and provides professional coaches for young people in state secondary schools.

He is currently launching his own charitable trust, 'Coaching4Free', to help people unable to afford professional coaching. He coaches face to face and by telephone.

Contact George at: GeorgeFMetcalfe@aol.com

WHAT'S STOPPING YOU ACHIEVING YOUR SUCCESS? WHAT WOULD HAPPEN IF YOU SAID HOW YOU REALLY FEEL? WHO SAID THAT YOU WEREN'T CONTRIBUTING HUGE VALUE?

BY MARTIN HAWORTH

It's amazing what the spark for change can be! From my work as a coach I'm going to share three questions with you, each of which was the spark for a different client. In these three fulfilling client relationships I was able to see through veneers of dissatisfaction and anxiety in a way that allowed opening up to new possibilities. It was that easy – the rest of the work the clients did themselves!

JEN

Jen came to me with a vision of her life. In a fairly extreme outpost of the UK, where women are still expected to be a mother and live within their extended family, she was on a mission. "Working Girl" with Melanie Griffiths is her inspiration and when we worked together it was clear she was driven.

At first, I worked as her boss and our working relationship, we both agreed, was professional and loyal to the organisation who employed us. As I was about to go off to become a coach on my own I promised to come back to her independently as soon as it was practical. We started working together three months later.

Jen has huge amounts of energy and drive. Very devoted to her young daughter, she wanted to escape from where her abilities were being paid lip service and to get fulfilment and reward. While she was seen as very good at her job, no regard was being paid to moving her on to achieve what she was really capable of.

She had other issues too. Married at 17 to her boyfriend who she had met at 14, she was now 34 and living in a numbing sort of relationship that could have gone on forever. Her husband resented her enthusiasm for her career, and where she lived she was seen as being above her station in life. He resented her confidence in herself and the gnawing ambition in her gut. As we worked together to build our working relationship, I became more and more sure that there was enormous potential for Jen; yet she was holding herself back. There was something that stopped her from making that leap of faith that would show her the way and make the difference.

One day, when she was talking with frustration about her domestic life, it became clear that her husband was sabotaging every attempt she was making to move forward. Jen was stuck in a negative environment which was pinning her down.

"What's stopping you achieving the success that Melanie Griffiths achieved in 'Working Girl'?" I asked her. She became very quiet. After what seemed like a couple of minutes silence but that in reality was less than 20 seconds, she said, "Well, nothing – only me, I suppose." We talked a little about what that meant and what she might be able to do to get herself out of the rut that described her life right now.

The following week when we met for our coaching call Jen told me excitedly that she had asked her husband to leave. He had done so and had already found himself a girlfriend. Jen and he had been married for 17 years.

Jen rapidly re-organised her life to accommodate being alone with her then 5 year old daughter. She rallied friends and family around and they were only too willing to help her. They told her that they couldn't understand what it was that had kept her in the relationship – and some of the less pleasant things they'd not been able to tell her about her husband's activities outside the relationship.

Jen has never looked back. In fact, now that she's divorced and has tried a new relationship of her own she is tentatively getting back into the world she hasn't experienced for nearly 20 years. Jen is taking her time and being selective, determined not to fall into the trap she fell into once before. It is a challenge for her, one she is very determined to overcome.

And her career? How is our 'Working Girl' progressing? Well, very successfully. Her career has spiralled. At first, she chose to stay with the organisation where she had begun her career all those years ago. New opportunities came her way and she excelled. She took on middle management roles as secondments and was perfect. Jen had amazing people skills and knew exactly where the balance was between familiarity with her people and drawing that line in the sand that delineates adequate managerial performance from exceptional. She did extremely well with every temporary position she undertook for the next year.

Yet they let her slip through their fingers. She was offered a redundancy package when her permanent role disappeared and she left them. She did it fearlessly (well, almost) and took on a number of interim consultancy roles, at which she excelled. People wanted more of her.

Despite this Jen felt that with a young daughter to support, she needed the security of a permanent role. She also realised that as well as being very capable technically in a role, she enjoyed working consistently with a group of people where she could make a significant impact strategically.

Jen missed two significant appointments, coming second out of an outstanding list of candidates. She was quite disappointed. She then applied for and was successful in an appointment which paid her double her previous salary. She had a temporary tactical role for three months and then moved into a role where she could influence change in a public organisation. She has flexitime and great pay. She works hard – too hard sometimes we agree – but she is very aware of how far she has come and also knows how far she can yet go.

Jen and I still work together and the goal now is to find someone to share her time with outside work. But she is in no hurry. She has also realised the learning from the experience with her ex-husband, with whom she has a good relationship. She will never fall into the same trap again. With coaching, she has made decisions for herself and explored solutions. She has grown. Rather than having to listen to friends and family who tried to tell her what she 'should' do, she answered the questions herself. This is the power of a coaching relationship. She sometimes speaks with horror about what her life might have been like if she had stopped herself achieving success any longer.

REBECCA

For Rebecca there was a different set of issues. She was a trained accountant and yet had never felt the urge to join the profession. Instead, she had joined the corporate sales world and had had a couple of jobs with world-leading organisations. But this wasn't quite right for her.

She joined a small team who provided training solutions to a niche of public bodies. Their focus was senior management in the different organisations and creating a programme of excellence to help them extend their skills. She was there for several years before I worked with them on a small seminar and then providing a coaching pilot. As part of the deal, Rebecca was offered a coaching session each month.

There is no doubt that she had an outstanding skill-set and while she was able to exploit that to a certain extent, her boss was very dynamic and assertive and there were times where they just didn't get on. Rebecca felt she was being overlooked.

This began to get in the way of her development and the frustration was beginning to show. On one call I asked her, "What would happen if you told her how you really feel?" Rebecca thought about that for a few moments and then said to me – "I'd be really scared to do that". I explained to her that if you express it like this, "I want to tell you how I feel about our relationship at the moment", there is no negative in the comment at all.

When put that way, she realised that this was going to be no attack on her boss. There was no description of **'you'** in the conversation, as it was all about Rebecca's **own** feelings. This usually takes a lot of the confrontation out of this sort of very open and honest conversation. And it was a conversation that she knew she had to have.

The Wednesday came and we had exchanged e-mails several times between our call and the dreaded day. We had joked a few times about a self-deprecating remark she often made of herself. "I'm just the wee girl" would come out when we started to talk about her aspirations. She had goals which she could dream about but rarely bring herself to believe were just around the corner.

Rebecca called me that evening. She had the conversation and it had gone very well. Her boss was aghast that her actions had led to one of her team to 'feel' that way about her work. It wasn't what her boss had perceived at all.

Rebecca went on to write an industry-changing training programme and spoke recently in a European conference in Paris. She is one of Europe's experts now in her field and she has emerged as a true star.

But things have changed even more. She decided to spend some time working as an Office Manager in an accountant's office to fine-tune her 'hands-on' people management skills. She was then approached by a business acquaintance to head up a new division providing HR consultancy solutions, which will expose her expertise to a wider range of potential clients. She receives double her salary from her previous role and is in seventh heaven. She is the "wee girl" no longer.

LUCIE

Of our 'Three Women', the last was the most astonishing. In fact I only worked with her for three months and only spoke to her 9 times.

Actually, by the start of the third call she had made a remarkable change in her life.

Lucie was a supervisor in a retail chain and was feeling rather undervalued. She came to me from a referral by a mutual friend who felt a little support might help her.

It was clear from the start that Lucie was very bright and extremely capable, but was short on self-esteem. Lucie didn't sell herself very well because she believed that she was of little importance. She managed a small team capably, but that had been as far as it had gone. She had applied for more senior roles but had been unsuccessful several times, almost always because her impact skills were lacking.

The opportunity to test who she was came quickly. After the second call she was to be at a meeting where her Regional Manager would be present. There would be several people there; her own manager, her Area Manager, other Supervisors and the Regional Manager. We discussed how she would usually behave in that meeting. She said that she would be quiet and say nothing. She had things to say, but she didn't feel they would be of value.

My question to her was around this. "Who **told you** that what you say isn't of value?" She answered slowly and quietly. "No-one." That was all she said.

We ended the call, with that hanging in the ether and she went off to her meeting.

103

On the next call she was electric. She had contributed positively to the meeting. After the meeting the Regional manager had asked her to show him around the Store and spoke with her for 30 minutes. He had never shown an interest in her before.

Lucie was offered a temporary management position two weeks later which she took and excelled in. She then decided that focus was not for her, but she took on a role as a store opener. She was then spotted by the head office and was interviewed for, and took the role of, a Regional Co-ordinator for store development. Her confidence bubbled all the time we worked together – after the second call. Sometimes she calls me to tell me how her career has progressed. Last Christmas she even looked me up and delivered a Christmas card personally.

Three women, three fairly simple questions and three very significant life changes.

Most importantly, these are three individuals who realised their potential and three individuals who are making much bigger contributions to their worlds.

About the Author

With a 20+ year career managing teams from 6 – 300 in a UK blue-chip organisation, Martin is a graduate of Newcastle College in the UK and CoachU, a leading US coach training organisation for whom he now trains a new generation of coaches. He is accredited both by the world's largest independent coaching accreditation body, the International Coach Federation and in **Intercept** a worldwide assessment tool which gives clients a better understanding of their unique strengths.

With a wide range of experience in the management coaching arena, Martin works primarily to ensure that his clients and their organisations achieve sustainable results with successful outcomes for all. His website, www.coaching-businesses-to-success.com is a very popular resource for executives, managers and small business owners which helps them, helps their people, helps their businesses grow.

Challenging, supportive and encouraging, Martin believes that everyone has untapped potential and his role is to facilitate his clients to make the very best of their careers and lives.

Learn more at: www.coaching-businesses-to-success.com

WHICH IS MORE IMPORTANT, HEALTH OR WEALTH?

BY STEVE HALLS

This is the question I always ask audiences at meetings, professional speaking engagements and with potential personal clients. I'm sure you know illness respects no financial boundaries. If you are not fit and healthy enough to enjoy your money, it could end up spent on medical expenses. Even worse, you might die with it. I believe we all get dealt certain cards in life. Some cards we cannot change because they are genetic, but some we *can* change through our lifestyle. Regardless of what life may throw at us, a fit and healthy body gives us a better chance of dealing with it successfully.

Time is a classic excuse for not looking after yourself. How many people do their emails on Sunday? How many of those go to the gym on Monday? Not many I can tell you for nothing. Why do we usually come off second best to work? How do we let a short-term business situation take precedence over a long term health mission? Yes, it beats me too.

I point out that no matter how successful you are, without health you are nothing. The individual has to take centre stage as the business develops around them, not ahead of them. Fitness is like an insurance policy for later life where you put a little in each week to reap the rewards when you are older. Now *that* business people *do* understand.

Some Life Coaches work with massive goals, but in my work I encourage clients to set big but achievable goals. They have to be realistic to be effective but a goal has to be a stretch. There must be a genuine sense of satisfaction when the goal is completed. That stimulates the mind and body to aim for something else. If a non-runner would like to complete a marathon, this would be seen as a big goal but achievable. If they wanted to do this within a week, well, you can see where this is going.

My starting point with a client is establishing where they are now. As when reading a map, if you don't know where you are, how can you know which way to go to reach your destination? We start with health checks such as: Blood Pressure, Resting Heart Rate, Lung Function and Body Fat %. I take Hip and Waist measurements along with any others that may help a particular client with their goals. I carry out fitness tests to establish their base level of fitness, so I can pitch the level of intensity when we start training.

This is 'benchmarking' and is vital for proving to yourself or your client that they are improving. It serves as a reality check when test results are not as expected. There is always an answer to why something either has or hasn't worked and in my experience it usually lies within the client and their commitment. Sometimes only when someone looks back will they see how much they've achieved. For instance, say last week they could complete 10 jumps, this week it is 12, then they can instantly see the improvement. If that figure was only nine, they might perceive this in a negative way. However, if I point out that they are jumping higher, this is progress too. They often don't see the improvement, but I do. That's the point of working with a coach. Coaches can see things the individual or team cannot.

Most of my work is with people who have tried and failed on numerous occasions to achieve their goals. These can be performance related goals or cosmetic ones such as weight loss/gain. A belief may get in their way. How many times have I heard: "I'm useless at swimming." or "I'm not built for running." or even "I'll never be able to do that"? Tackling people's beliefs in their abilities is important in my job. If somebody is not as proficient at running as they would like, it could be for numerous reasons, even something as simple as never having been shown how to run properly.

Questions I always ask someone who says they are a poor runner are: "Who says you are a poor runner?" and "What would make you a good runner? Give me a standard..." If they say they want to run faster, I could be pedantic and ask: "How fast do you run at the moment?" I could also ask: "If you're a bad runner, what makes a good runner?" The client has to think outside the box and come up with what they interpret as good running. For one client being a good runner meant running 10 miles without getting out of breath. So, does she think that some of the world's top class sprinters are poor runners? I'll leave that with you.

Breaking down a belief in sport can be easier than breaking down one in life because I can usually prove to a client very quickly that their belief is dubious or unfounded. Once I've rocked the foundation of a previous belief it opens the door for more unhelpful beliefs to be smashed into oblivion.

Medical conditions play an enormous part in my work. Most of my clients have a debilitating condition which prevents them from doing particular activities. This could be anything from muscle strain to a "full grown big bad medical nightmare" (Technical Term).

One such client had so many issues she had given up doing anything about it. The intervention of her son, who bought her a very kind present of 10 sessions, dramatically changed her life. She was 4'11"and weighed over 21 stone. She was unable to stand longer than a few seconds and was totally reliant on her wheelchair. She had Arthritis in her knee and took 8 strong painkillers a day. She is manic depressive and on medication to keep her calm. Her blood sugar level was sometimes 27mmol/litre of blood, showing she was diabetic. A hopeless case? I think not. A challenge, but like all challenges if you break it down into component parts and deal with them individually, it becomes easier.

I began by getting her complete trust and tackling her most fearful issue. She was terrified of falling over because she knew full well she was not strong enough to get back up again. I gave her a series of exercises to build the muscles for standing. We coupled this with a plan of action for using surrounding objects to assist her and overcame this problem quite quickly. The constant pain in her knee made it uncomfortable getting down on the floor, but the desired outcome was more important than the immediate pain.

Weight loss was the next priority as it was causing so many of her problems. When someone does not move they burn few calories. This had to be reversed. We worked on the leg muscles to make them strong enough for walking. Within two weeks, she achieved her first goal, walking across the road outside her house for the first time since she moved there 4 years previously. In fact she had moved there because she could no longer manage stairs. With a regular training session, swimming and a careful eye on the calories she lost more than 6 stone over two years.

The difference in her life has been incredible. She has not suffered from Arthritis in her knee for over a year and does not take painkillers. Her blood sugar level has reduced to under 6mmol/litre of blood, enabling her to reduce her medication by over 2/3. She no longer has to see the specialist, dietician or psychiatrist and is now so confident that she is chairperson of a voluntary mental health group giving support to others. She knows there is still much to do, but her story is an inspiration to any client I work with. Proof was in the pudding in the winter when she fell over in the snow. Everybody around made a fuss and prepared for the worst but she leapt up and carried on as if nothing had even happened. She jogs round sports pitches now.

This is the power of good exercise and diet. This isn't about the trainer (although I do take credit – with modesty of course) but the lifestyle you choose. I show people real life incidences of what happens if you choose this path.

Motivation is very individual. While some are motivated by the benefits they will get, others are motivated by the consequences of not doing something. Establishing which type a client is and working with that is what I have found to be best. A lot of trainers spend energy trying to change the client's behaviour instead of using the natural resources the client already has. If the client's behaviours are not serving them well it could be their existing methods of motivation preventing them from achieving their goal.

Some clients see a personal goal as very selfish. Right they are! And that's the way it should be. If they feel uncomfortable with that, I find out what they like doing for others. That might seem strange, but it does get results. An example would be someone who has neglected their health but loves to help out at the local school. They are too busy to do exercise for their own health but will give every last minute to others. Given the question: "How much more could you give the school if you were fitter and felt more energetic?" The most stubborn person will admit that they could do more. There's the motivational factor. I recall what they would do with the extra energy and remind them of that. So now what stops them? -That's the really selfish part.

Many clients want to lose weight and have tried every diet going. Why have they failed? I tend not to advise on specific diets other than eating 'wholefoods' where possible, in correct amounts (for more details, see my 90 Day 'Fit Body Initiative') What I do concentrate on is their motivation for getting their weight down. "Fit people are generally not fat." I tell them, and we chase the fitness. Believe me, when they get fit the weight comes down. As they feel fitter and stronger they increase their workload, burning more and more calories daily.

Keeping a positive mental attitude is very important for personal fitness and weight loss. You can train to get better, stronger, fitter, or thinner but to do that you have to get outside your comfort zone. We live in a "want it now" society. Everything is instant. That's no different when it comes to health and fitness. I am amazed at headlines in fitness magazines promising a "perfect body in 6 weeks" or "great abdominals in 14 days". I find it a constant battle with clients who expect that these sorts of result are the norm. Fitness takes time. Gradual improvements are all that is required to get you to your desired outcome. Patience is the key.

Good self-esteem is also a key in personal motivation. If I ask a client how they feel and they say "Not bad, okay I suppose." I turn their slight negativity into positivity. I say, "You look great. Why not say you look great?" It takes practice to love yourself unconditionally, because people don't like to be seen as arrogant. I don't think it is arrogance to be positive and appreciate that you are getting fitter, feeling better and looking good.

The techniques I use depend on the type of person. With an overweight person I use visualisation to help them see what the future holds. A definite picture in their head of what they will look like serves as a great motivator for training hard. With someone suffering from Anorexia, I use facts. If asked: "How big are you?" They normally respond with a figure wildly off the truth. I show them their imagination is far from the actual reality and that is the starting point of my work with them.

Believing a client can do something can help them to believe in themselves. They do the doubting: I do the questioning and instil belief in their ability. The best examples of this are the "How far...?How fast...?" type of questions. If I know a client wants to improve their swimming, I will ask, "How far can you swim under water?" This assumes the client can swim under water. Already they are thinking positively, searching their mind for how far they can swim underwater. My belief in their ability straight away instils confidence so they only have to think positively of a performance related task and not whether they can do it at all. This type of questioning is widely used by NLP (Neuro Linguistic Programming) Practitioners and does not allow for the client to think "I can't". I have found this works very successfully in fitness coaching.

All people, regardless of ability can improve with good coaching. Not all of my clients are restricted by physical or mental issues. Top sportsmen need help too. If they have a weakness in their sport, I analyse the movements they carry out and break them down into components. By working on individual parts to eliminate weaknesses, you can build up again to make the whole much stronger. Sometimes their weaknesses are more mental than physical. I then have to eliminate the doubts in much the same way as a life coach would.

I have found through the years that many people require some sort of coaching – physical or otherwise. However, fitness coaching can only be practiced on clients presenting themselves for coaching! Unfortunately, too many successful and go-getting entrepreneurs never give themselves the opportunity to improve their health and fitness. Hopefully, thanks to this chapter, you're not one of them.

About the Author

Born and bred in Stoke-on-Trent England, I joined the British Army straight from school at 16 where I served for more than 23 years. I attained the rank of Warrant Officer Class 1 before I left in 2000. On leaving the Army, I passed the Premier Diploma Course in Fitness Training and Sports Therapy.

My speciality is working with people with special medical conditions. These people provide me with my biggest challenges, which inspire me further. I do have my fair share of people with no special issues other than the desire and somewhat lack of motivation to get fit and healthy. Somewhere in all this, there is a place for everyone. No person is excluded regardless of age or ability.

In 2004 I became the Director of Fitness for the Academy of High Achievers who deliver awe-inspiring personal development courses throughout the UK. It was the meeting of such inspirational people on these courses that inspired me to write my renowned "Fit Body Initiative" eCourse and book. This is a 90-day fitness programme designed to get you on the road to a fit and healthy lifestyle by providing you with information, tips and a daily call to action via your email. The exercises build up into the best training programme money can buy. It is like having your own Personal Trainer alongside you every step of the way.

In 2005 I became a Certified Professional Speaker and have been delivering unique and fun keynote speeches on Health and Fitness. I'm married to Marie and my hobbies include folk singing and playing the guitar to any misguided person mad enough to want to listen.

For more details of my products, services and background visit my website: www.stevehalls.co.uk

Judy Barber

WHAT WILL YOUR PERFECT BUSINESS BE LIKE?

BY GÉRARD JAKIMAVICIUS

It's not just business. It is personal!

Welcome to everyone with even a slight interest in business. The principles here apply to one-man start-ups, to global corporates and to public bodies. They apply to managers, business owners and board directors.

This chapter consists of a logical series of key questions I might ask my business clients. Each client is individual and unique: businesses are at different stages with different challenges and opportunities. Flexibility is required. Nevertheless, every individual in a commercial enterprise will need to know the answer to these business questions ... if they are to flourish in a dynamic market place!

Not all questions to my business clients are about business as one of my main aims is to coach holistically. Personal issues like fear, risk aversion, emotional attachment and ego can block business and work progress, and questions about the individual weave into a careful process of moving both personal and business issues forward.

In this chapter we will deal with the business stuff only, but understanding that business coaching is always more involved than just asking business questions.

My style is such that sorting out business challenges is often fun. The principles are serious and the implications are serious but progress can be full of choices and fun.

We'll start with the end in mind – a clear vision based upon your personal values and aims.

Imagine you owned or ran a business and it was running perfectly – what would your business look like?

The vision is an end point which takes note of how you operate today *and* of whether you are heading in the right direction. It should be the first step of a Business Plan, so let's see how it fits into the Business Planning Process.

What are the fundamental steps to consider in running your business?

Imagine an "ultra filled" sandwich. The massive filling is your Marketing Strategy and the bottom slice of bread is your foundation or why you are in business, including your vision. The top slice of bread is your processes and operating systems, how you run your business. This analogy is a neat way of looking at a Business Plan.

THE SANDWICH

The bottom slice (visioning, reasoning and selection)

Why are you going into business? What do you want to get out of it? This is so basic as to seem daft – but any lack of clarity now may have major repercussions. Making money is not a "full" enough answer – why do you want to make money? Keep drilling to test the core of what is driving you. When you get an answer keep drilling down by asking "why?" This often leads to the core reason and an "aha" moment!

What am I good at and what do I enjoy? Looking back on ultra-fulfilling moments in your past can often give you some real clues.

- What different services or products shall I offer? You have such enormous choices, each with a multitude of variations, so exactly why are you choosing this one?

- If you are already in business, you can ask the following gems:

  o What was offered originally, and why? What is offered now, and why? How would you like this offering to evolve in the coming years?

  o Is your vision of where you want your business to go clear? The world changes daily, so your vision from even a year ago might have changed dramatically – are you clear about that vision today?

- o Is your vision today relevant to what is happening in your company? Is it relevant to what is happening in the market place? By that I mean customers' present demands and competitor activity.

- o Is it relevant to what is happening in the world at large? By that I mean: does it take into account **P**olitical, **E**conomic, **S**ocial, **T**echnological, **L**egal and **E**nvironmental aspects (a useful check known as **PESTLE**)?

Finding what people are passionate about can be a great base for going into business.

There is a growing trend towards people starting their business with a "moral" basis such as environmental responsibility embedded within how the company is run. An example would be valuing equal opportunities because people believe in this rather than because they have to comply with regulations.

Ensuring your personal values are expressed within a vision or mission statement can be helpful.

I always challenge my clients around their vision. This helps either confirm even more powerfully that their original vision was right for them, or, more frequently, they define their vision in better words and with new accuracy – very empowering. Sometimes people realise their original vision is not what they want at all and need to find what they really want instead.

To be successful you need to support your passion with all the tried and tested disciplines of a business.

My own business coaching vision includes inspiring thousands of people to run businesses that give them immense pleasure, great results and improve the world around them.

The 'filling' (Marketing Strategy)

What is your target market? This is the easiest question to ask, but the hardest to answer. Who might want your product or service and why? Who do you want to focus on and who should you leave out?

What are all the sectors in that market? People buy from you for different reasons. In one retailing role I calculated there were at least 6 customer types/reasons why people bought sandwiches. The business person with 5 minutes to dash out for a sandwich is in a different mode from an old lady who wants to browse. It is vital to understand different sectors really well. It may be the hardest step, but it is also the key one. Understanding your potential customers is everything!

What are the needs of these sectors? The needs could be similar, but often vary enormously between apparently similar sectors. It is vital those needs are understood. It affects the ways in which you market your wares. This is crucial for staying in business.

Where are each of these sectors? You may need to do clever market research here, perhaps with the aid of a specialist company. Getting this right is well worth it and could save a fortune in untargeted advertising and promotion.

How can you effectively get in touch with these sectors?

What language do they use? I mean specific words, phrases, jargon, abbreviations, buzz words and topics.

What is happening in the market place? How do you best respond? You can view this big task as exploration.

What is the competition doing, and what might they do? How do you best respond?

Given all the above, how will you make your product or service better and different from what is currently in the market place?

How will you effectively communicate your price and brand?

The 'filling' tells you that you need a clear and well thought through Marketing Strategy. It can take time and be challenging until you get it right. Once you have a coherent Marketing Strategy look at the Marketing Tactics – for example advertising and networking. Strategy and Tactics need checking and updating as your business performs and develops.

The top slice (Systems)

What pre-delivery systems do you require? These keep the office running smoothly and are all related to provision of the product or service. They are crucial to the efficiency of the whole operation Examples are phone systems, bookkeeping, health and safety, office and staff facilities.

What delivery systems do you require? This covers everything directly connected to making and delivering sales. Crucially, this must cover how you measure and manage customer satisfaction. This is perhaps the most overlooked aspect in businesses. Managers often think that talking and listening to their customers is enough. Wrong, wrong, wrong! I am passionate about this. Businesses of all sizes need to understand what their customers really think about the whole experience. They need the whole picture not just what comes out in a friendly chat! The information needs collating and actioning.

How are you capturing the learning as you go along? Have you looked across the horizons and challenged yourself to learn all the lessons that are waiting to help you move forward?

How can you best do it?

How can you incorporate your learning?

If you can't do everything then what comes first?

We know a perfect sandwich has two good tasty pieces of bread and an exquisite filling that is perfect for the bread ... just like an effective Business Plan!

Now you are up and running, what next?

Maintenance

Do you use these questions in starting up, and then forget them once they are in place?

I am sure you are saying "definitely no". The world is not standing still, nor are your customers or competitors. Maintenance must be ongoing and cyclical to get you where you and your business need to be. It is an image that helps you holistically check all the high level issues involved in running a business.

How do you know you are on track?

Measure your business. How and what do you measure and how frequently?

You could be appear to be doing well, but are you? For example, sales could be going well, but profits may be being eroded by reaching the wrong client base.

How do you keep a balanced view for today and the future?

Keep referring to your original vision, check where you are and what's going on around you. Update the vision if necessary.

How can you ensure you keep what you actually do in line with the values of the business?

If you are a sole trader or the only owner, there is likely to be a strong correlation between what you do and what you believe and value.

When decision making involves others how can you avoid conflicts of values?

The Big Twist

What do you measure?

Are you ready for this, because here's the big twist!

Most companies measure pretty well only the financial stuff.

Is it is only money that counts in achieving success?

Aren't most financial measures historical?

Financial parameters are vital but:

What about the people?

Start with the customer.

Consider the core of most businesses – the staff. What are their needs?

Are there shareholders to consider?

What about other stakeholders?

So, how will you ensure all these different people are kept happy?

How will you:

- know if they are happy?

- know what they really think?
- know their needs and wants?

What are the different ways in which your company could work?

Here are further questions about this aspect of your business:

What are the processes involved in running this business?

How efficiently do the processes run now?

Could you run the business with different processes?

Underneath the processes are systems and procedures. We can ask the same questions as for processes.

What different levels of measurements will you set up?

It can be helpful to distinguish between high-level measurements called Key Performance Indicators which tell you how the whole business is doing and where it is going, and lower level day-to-day Operating Measures. Distinguishing these two level of measures can be especially helpful in large organisations, or where the structure or offer is complex .

What you measure, to get a balanced picture of what is happening holistically across the company, and whether this is taking you towards your reality-checked vision leads us to these questions:

- What do you measure?

- What do you measure it against?

- Has it been benchmarked against the best in the industry?

- How frequently do you measure?

- Who decides actions and who implements the action plan?

Parting Message

I have shown you a holistic approach applicable to any business, with key questions to ask. It is based on a robust 'sandwich' Business Planning Process – with Marketing Strategy as the filling. Logical supporting questions ensure all major, high level, aspects are considered. It is not just about your business thinking, but about you and what is important to you. You have many options from which to choose and many decisions to make along the way.

The journey you undertake in a business will offer you opportunities to grow and is very much about your personal development.

As a business owner, manager or a team leader you will have the opportunity, and responsibility, for developing others. Through coaching questions you have opportunities to assist, support and challenge people around you.

Running a business enables business owners and employees to earn a livelihood and to be in an arena for personal fulfilment.

So, as I said at the beginning, it's not just about business. It is personal!

Once you know the steps ensure you enjoy the journey!

About the Author

Gérard was born in France, on what is now the site of EuroDisney - which might explain much!

He has over 25 years successful commercial experience across Europe, covering many functions; this enables him to quickly assess the issues in companies and organisations.

In 1999 he set up Life Coach Associates, which delivers both business and personal coaching to clients. He is a graduate of the world renowned Coach U.

Whether they require business or personal coaching, Gérard coaches clients from a holistic viewpoint. We are all unique individuals who need to balance all aspects of our life to attain calm and achieve our best.

Coaching Business

His vision is helping thousands of clients run successful businesses in which the owners feel a real sense of control, and which have a positive impact on the world around them.

His clients include start-up business owners, employees and corporate executives. SME owners seem particularly drawn to Gerard's coaching.

Coaching Style

Gérard's coaching style is to initially guide the client to check their vision, and even to challenge and enhance it. The current client situation is considered in context to allow them to see where they really are.

Clients are then encouraged to tap into their own creativity (usually finding levels they did not know they had) to develop options on how to move forward. If the client is ready, this often involves taking leaps rather than little steps.

Helping the client to set up their own plan to attain their goals, and monitoring progress, keeps the client on track while gaining energy and confidence to increase their pace.

Vitally, all goals are respected, no matter how serious or personal. Yet Gérard's style is to have lots of fun with the client in attaining those goals.

Learn more at: www.life-coach-associates.com

Judy Barber

PART FOUR: AN IMPORTANT CAUTION

Joe Armstrong's contribution comes in at a different angle with a chapter title that is not a question but a warning. He puts questioning in a context, and so I have put it in the middle of the book. He isn't, obviously, saying that we should never ask a question again, but that we should look carefully at the context of the conversation and remember how important it is to listen.

Judy Barber

QUESTIONS SHOULD COME WITH A GOVERNMENT HEALTH WARNING

BY JOE ARMSTRONG

Thomas Gordon's famous book Parent Effectiveness Training (Random House, 1970, 2000) lists twelve blocks to listening. The eleventh category of blocks to listening is 'probing, questioning and interrogating'! Probing questions, as in 'really good questions' are an example of not listening. Hence this cautionary chapter in a book on great questions to ask!

His full list of blocks to listening is as follows:

Ordering, directing, commanding, warning, admonishing, threatening, exhorting, moralizing, preaching, advising, giving solutions or suggestions, lecturing, teaching, giving logical arguments, judging, criticising disagreeing, blaming, praising, agreeing, name-calling, ridiculing, shaming, interpreting, diagnosing, reassuring, sympathising, consoling, supporting, probing, questioning, interrogating, withdrawing, distracting, humouring, diverting.

It's so interesting to look at those blocks to listening. When you first read that list you're struck by things that you never thought of before as not listening. For instance, consoling, praising, advising, sympathising, and, of course, questioning, probing and interrogating. In short, when we ask a question – even a brilliant question – we've stopped listening.

I'd like to give you an example of this from my own life. When I was a student for the Roman Catholic priesthood – I studied for nine years but chose to leave before ordination – I elected to do some counselling to help me to decide whether or not to stay on the priestly path. I remember asking the counsellor: "Do you think I have a vocation?"

She chose to teach me an important lesson by her reply. "Yes I do," she said. And then, some moments later, "No, I don't". She watched my response to both replies. Her "Yes, I do/No I don't" dual response also showed me my need to decide for myself irrespective of anybody else's opinion. I alone must make and live with this decision! Notice that the counsellor's wise ploy at this stage didn't involve a question at all.

Then she asked: "How long have I known you?" We'd had less than twenty sessions together so she had known me less than twenty hours. With her question she had reflected back to me the folly of me, who had lived in my body, mind and gut feelings for twenty seven years, considering that another person, who had known me for perhaps only seventeen hours, could know me better than I knew myself.

It was the best thing she did for me. She had so effectively reflected back to me the silliness of what I had thought and done in asking her if I had a priestly vocation.

She went further. Before getting to her point, she thanked me effusively for giving her the power to make such an important decision for the life of someone else. Of course, she was play-acting – though she acted really well. She said: "Thank you so much. You have given me so much power over you. Wow! It feels great!" Then she went on: "But take back that power because it is not mine to have. It is yours." I could not have asked for a better counsellor. She had just demonstrated for me that I alone could make this decision. She did ask me one other good question which helped me to get out of my head. "What does your gut say?" I am a gut person rather than a head person. That was a great question to ask. Once I got out of my head, I faced the fact that, if I had to decide on the basis of my gut, I'd leave. And leave I did.

This brings me to the word 'conscience'. I define it as 'my honest judgment', which I consider to be the best definition of conscience. We are each born with a purpose. We are called to become ourselves and to fulfil our higher purpose. My counsellor helped me to see that I needed to make my honest judgment, not to lean on her judgement or anyone else's.

Often we procrastinate and stay on the fence, terrified of making our authentic decision. We fear it might be the wrong decision. It can seem easier not to decide or to let someone else decide for us, whether that be an authority or significant other. That way, we feel we can blame them if it goes wrong. But when we accept our adult responsibility there is no one to 'blame' but ourselves. And that is the essence of personal responsibility. It is also the tenet of maturity, courage and self-actualisation. In my view relatively few people do that.

In talking about conscience as *my honest judgment*, it is a *judgment* that is at issue, and not a feeling nor a little voice in my head, nor an expert's view, including religious or even legal authorities. In forming an honest judgment I'm aware of the human propensity to fool oneself. One can be prejudiced, biased and lazy. Sometimes we don't follow through or we skip steps. Within the Christian tradition there is talk of sinfulness and blindness. In the secular world we talk of being in a rush to judge, being prejudiced – that is, literally, to pre-judge. That's why it is helpful to be clear about what 'my honest judgment' means.

In short, when it is genuinely my own, when it is not a feeling or a rule or from an authority, when it is honest, when I have taken the trouble to ask all the questions, when I'm conscious of my own biases and my propensity to fool myself, then it can be an act of conscience. When I have taken all that on board it is I and I alone who must make the judgment.

Once I've made my honest judgement, not only may I act on it but I am obliged to do so. Not to act on it would be to become inauthentic and act in bad faith. So, if it is my honest judgment that I should break a law then not only may I but I must! For instance, if I am abjectly poor and you are a billionaire and my family will die for lack of food unless I rob you, and if it is my honest judgement that it is the right course of action for me, then not only may I rob you but I must do so!

As part of the process of coming to my own honest judgment I must inform myself of laws and the views of authorities and experts, but the decision is still my own. My honest judgment is mine and mine alone. If I judge differently from the law or the Pope or the Queen, so be it. I follow my conscience and break the law. Of course, I must accept the consequences for doing so, which may include going to prison or having to pay a fine or, in another age, being exiled to a far flung colony.

In working one to one with people we are seeking to facilitate them to become so internally strong that they can act in accordance with their conscience, even when this violates their normal behaviour or the culture or sub-culture into which they were born or still live in. We want to foster within them the inner strength to know and act from their authentic self.

Imagine how life could be if everyone followed their conscience. I think it is important in working with people to help them to come to that kind of inner and outer strength. Asking *"What is your gut feeling?"* at the right moment can help. But not asking anything at all and simply reflecting back what the client has asked – such as do I have a vocation and the folly of expecting someone else other than the self to be able to answer it – is the best of all.

About the Author

Joe Armstrong is happiest being described as a human being. He has graduate degrees in philosophy, English and history, and in theology. He taught English and religious education for five years in London's East End and has been a professional writer, journalist, author and editor for more than 10 years. He's author of "Write Way to Stop Smoking", a guided programme to stop smoking and other addictions which you can get online at www.bookshaker.com or www.amazon.co.uk and "Men's Health – the Common Sense Approach", which has been translated into several languages. Joe lives with his wife and two children in the Irish countryside. He can be contacted by email: joearmstrong@eircom.net

PART FIVE: METAPHORS AND MIRACLES

These chapters use imagery and imagination. What have bells, firewalks, spinning and miracles in common? - thinking of them asks for an imaginative stretch, which is a common thread here. Wendy Sullivan writes about metaphors that clients use, Sanjay Shah about a firewalk as a metaphor, Tony Burgess about consciously 'spinning' the feeling of magnificence and Jamie Smart asks us to consider the results of a miracle.

How can you use *your* imagination to contribute to life?

Judy Barber

AND WHAT WOULD YOU LIKE TO HAVE HAPPEN?

BY WENDY SULLIVAN

Do you have meetings that go in circles? With your child, do you both repeat your own take on things, without 'hearing' each other or finding a way forward? Do you sometimes find yourself getting stuck when working with someone? Do clients sometimes return having not maintained the changes they made? This chapter shows you the basics of working with groups and individuals in a way that might get different results – and you're not expected to have answers, just the questions.

Here are core concepts, examples and an activity to do. Bear in mind different contexts in your life and consider how you could use these ideas.

"And what would you like to have happen?" focuses on a desired outcome. Most clients focus on problems, so this question invites them to think of what they really want instead. It shines light on aspects of experience that may have been languishing in a dark corner, seldom visited, and largely unknown.

When asked: "And what would you like to have happen?", someone is likely to discover new information. As questioning continues, the client discovers further new information, and learns. Then you can facilitate the realisation of what needs to happen for them to achieve their desired outcome. Change may start happening right away. And because the change comes entirely from them, it will be consistent with who they are and be a perfect 'fit'. This makes long-lasting change more achievable.

This good experience is not what usually happens when we communicate however. Why? It is because we are 'meaning-making' beings and so when someone begins to talk we begin making assumptions to fill the gaps in our knowledge so we can 'make sense' of what they say. It is easy to forget that we don't actually know this information to be true: by 'making sense' we're merely making assumptions. Our assumptions then lead us to believe that we know the answers to their problems, and so we offer advice. However good our advice may be, it is unlikely to fit their experience.

While running 'Train the Trainer' courses, I have had participants who said they were nervous about training. It is easy to assume they want to feel confident and to give advice on how to look/be more confident: "Stand solidly on both feet to be well-grounded.", "Make eye contact with your participants." etc. But on being asked, "And what would you like to have happen?" they said:

"I need techniques for dealing with difficult participants."

"I'd be fine if I could work out how to get the content clear in my mind."

"I want my face to stay normal (not blush)."

"I want to enjoy training."

My advice might have been good in general, but it wouldn't have helped these people to achieve their desired outcomes.

This approach involves asking questions that allow people to gain new information about their experience of life. The only words the coach uses are the client's words, and a few carefully designed questions that help the client to keep finding out more about how they are structuring their experience. This sets the stage for them to learn and for change to happen more effectively than if the coach had provided some 'off-the-shelf' advice or technique.

Resisting the temptation of giving advice, and honouring the client's choice of words rather than paraphrasing, come from David Grove, a psychotherapist who developed Clean Language when working with people who had suffered trauma. He found if he kept his own words to himself and just repeated the client's words back to them, and asked questions that added very few assumptions, clients were able to explore their experience and learn from it in ways that allowed them to move on.

This approach is 'clean' because the coach keeps advice, assumptions and solutions to themselves. The coach regards the client as the expert regarding themselves, while the coach is expert in directing the client's attention to aspects of their experience that will help them learn. Any changes the client then makes are the result of their own development.

As the coach, you are largely invisible. This is not everyone's cup of tea: it can be fun having people say how wonderful your suggestions are! The pay-back is experiencing how the client's change happens for them. There is always a wonderful logic to the changes. In retrospect you can spot clues that were there from the start but there is no shortcut: the changes emerge from going through the process.

What else needs to be in a conversation that includes "And what would you like to have happen?" ?

There are four elements:

1. Exquisite attention paid to the client

The coach needs to attend exquisitely to what the client says and does, in order to remember exact words and gestures since these fill the 'x' and 'y' slots that customise the questions.

2. 'Clean Language' questions developed by David Grove

"And what would you like to have happen?" gets the session started. The client's desired outcome may change. By asking the question again periodically you ensure you are working from the latest update.

To help the client explore aspects of their current perception, use additional Clean Language questions. The core questions are:

- "And what kind of x is that x?"
- "And is there anything else about x?"
- "And where/whereabouts is x?"
- "And that's x like what?"
- "And is there a relationship between x and y?"
- "And when x, what happens to y?"
- "And then what happens? / What happens next?"
- "And what happens just before x?"
- "And where could/does x come from?"

3. Metaphor

> "Metaphor is the process of 'understanding and experiencing one kind of thing in terms of another'"
> **Lakoff and Johnson**
>
> "Metaphor, that's how the whole fabric of mental interconnections holds together. Metaphor is right at the bottom of being alive."
> **Gregory Bateson**
>
> Examples of metaphors...
>
> There's light at the end of the tunnel.
> ('light', 'tunnel' and 'end' are metaphorical)
>
> I want to get clear about which path to take.
> ('clear', 'path' and 'take' are metaphorical, unless it's a real path)
>
> I need to get into the right mood.
> (Where 'mood' is a container that I can 'get into').

People have a natural tendency to use metaphors when they explore experience. You can facilitate this by not adding 'dirty' comments, questions, opinions or views into the mix.

Someone's metaphors have a similar structure to the experience that they are considering. In addition, metaphors condense information and make things more tangible, so it is easier for client and coach to work in metaphor, rather than conceptually.

Clean Language questions can, however, also be used when someone is talking conceptually. I remember a coachee who was new to managing client accounts. He was an excellent project manager and very task-focused. He was unconvinced about his ability, and the need, to attend to relationships in his new job. He talked conceptually saying, "This job is like the Project Management job I had. I was good at it and I'm angry my Manager now evaluates me as mediocre." I asked Clean Language questions and, after some time, he said he wanted to "Throw a rope across the river". Using this metaphor we explored how he wanted to build work relationships making sure the rope was securely anchored on the shore, asking for help to anchor it on the other side, weaving more ropes together to make it stronger. He discovered what actions he needed to take in the real world to build relationships with his clients (fortunately without real ropes!).

He applied his knowledge and as a result was not made redundant in the next round of cuts.

As with this man, changes happening within the client's metaphor landscape are likely to translate into changes in the real world, because their structure is similar.

4. A modelling attitude

The coach asks questions so the client can make a mental 'model' of what their experience is like. The facilitator also makes a model in their mind of what the client tells them and uses this model to decide what to focus the client's attention on next.

Clean Language, metaphor and modelling make up Symbolic Modelling, developed by James Lawley and Penny Tompkins, after they had modelled David Grove's use of Clean Language. We are focusing mainly on the Clean Language questions here and it is their use alongside metaphor and modelling that supercharges the experience for the client.

How Might You Use These Principles?

The Clean Language approach is being used more and more widely to help people achieve their desired outcomes. Some applications include:

Team Building

I worked with a virtual team to help them improve how they worked together. Everyone was asked what they would like to have happen regarding how the team worked. One said he wanted them to be like a formula one pit crew team. Someone else wanted it to be like setting sail for distant shores. Needless to say, these two people had been having a hard time working together! The other people's metaphors were all different and equally revealing.

As each team member was facilitated by others to develop their metaphor, there were nods and smiles as the team realised they had seen individuals 'living' their metaphors from day to day. For example, the 'Formula One' person's meetings had no 'pit stops' for lunch or tea. People were expected to keep working and concentrating as long as there was work to do. He spoke fast, frequently losing team members who couldn't grasp concepts flashing past at high speed.

During that meeting, people started changing their communication so their response to an individual was given within the logic and spirit of the metaphor of that individual. For example, when talking to the 'Formula One' person: "If we take this new tightly-targeted approach, we'd get it done much faster and we'd beat the other divisions by miles. We'd have to do meticulous planning before we start, and have a practice run." This helped members to feel understood. They were also more understanding of how and why others responded differently to situations affecting the team.

Developing a Mission or Vision

Clean Language can help communities, groups and teams develop shared understandings of what they want to achieve and how to go about it.

I was in a team facilitating members of a spiritual community to discover more about a key part of their mission. By the end they reported having a better understanding of it as a community. Individuals not only had more knowledge about how they could contribute to it, but were living it day-to-day in ways others could identify.

Changing The Ethos Of An Organisation

I was in a team working with an organisation offering weight loss classes. Class leaders were taught Clean Language skills to help them aid members in becoming motivated to lose weight. The results have been such that they are also encouraging managers to attend Clean Language training. They appreciate that this approach to communication, motivation and leading change has a part to play in many contexts of organisational life.

Modelling Good Practice

I carried out an NHS project exploring how clinicians, skilled in relating well to patients, do what they do. We found they had metaphors that unconsciously guided them, for example being a 'chameleon blending into the patient's world', or conducting a 'South East Asian Business Meeting' (conversation, doing business, further conversation).

After responding to a few Clean Language questions, their awareness was raised enough for them to consciously further improve the way they related. In one instance this significantly raised the clinician's job satisfaction. In another instance a doctor changed the way he taught practical work so junior doctors could use this approach to build their rapport skills too.

Relating well is very important to patient outcomes and I hope this project will be the foundation for further training to help clinicians relate well to patients.

Interviewing

The Police in some areas now ask Clean Language questions when interviewing vulnerable witnesses so that it cannot be said that they lead the witnesses.

An Activity For You: Developing A 'Blueprint Of Excellence':

If you are reading this you are probably interested in being at the cutting edge of communication. You might like to use Clean Language questions to develop a metaphor of what it is like when you are listening at your best. You could do this alone or with a friend.

Ask yourself: "When I am listening at my best, that is like what?" For example, it might be like:

- A bright spotlight illuminating the speaker, and nothing distracts you from them.
- A heart to heart connection.
- Their voice rings out loud and clear and other sounds are muffled.

Probably for you it is quite different from these examples. Whatever it is like is fine.

Then ask yourself any/all the Clean Language questions above, in any order. Feel free to re-use questions. For example, using the example metaphors above, questions could be:
"And when it is like a bright spotlight, where is that spotlight?"

"And when it's like heart to heart connection, is there anything else about that connection?"

"And when it rings out loud and clear, what kind of clear is that clear?"

As you discover more about your blueprint for listening, consider whether there are previously unspotted opportunities in everyday life for listening this way (and perhaps also asking some Clean Language questions).

Consider asking the other person "And what would you like to have happen?" It is a powerful question that can help individuals and teams feel acknowledged and respected, so they are empowered to make full use of their amazing abilities to achieve desired outcomes for themselves, their communities and the world.

> When telling others about this work, please also credit David Grove for 'Clean Language', and Penny Tompkins and James Lawley for 'Symbolic Modelling'.

About the Author

Wendy helps individuals and groups identify changes in thinking or behaviour that make a difference. She then supports them in making those changes in the real world, so that they achieve their goals. This invariably involves communication and relationship skills. These abilities underpin personal effectiveness in a world where we all form one system and all have an impact on each other: little is achieved without the involvement or assistance of others.

Wendy has worked as a Speech and Language Therapist and NLP (Neuro Linguistic Programming) trainer and has extensive involvement with Clean Language and Symbolic Modelling. She coaches, facilitates and trains internationally with individuals and organisations.

She believes that when you attend exquisitely to people, as with Clean Language, it gives them the chance to do their very best thinking, problem-solving and goal-achieving. They will then be more able to attend exquisitely to others... and if those who can do so, pay attention and ask a few good questions, the benefits will keep cascading out. It seems an easy way to improve everyone's lives.

Wendy runs a training and development company, Discovery Works Ltd www.discovery-works.co.uk

She also offers training in Clean Language and Symbolic Modelling and runs free teleclasses for newcomers to sample Clean Language,

and to experience asking and being asked Clean Language questions...
www.smallchangecompany.com

Wendy is writing an introductory book about Clean Language for publication next year.

She is indebted to Penny Tompkins, James Lawley and David Grove for their generosity in supporting her learning and development. Read more about Symbolic Modelling and Clean Language at www.cleanlanguage.co.uk and in James and Penny's book 'Metaphors in Mind'.

Judy Barber

ARE YOU IN A PLACE OF I CAN OR I CAN'T?

BY SANJAY SHAH

 There's an affirmation at the heart of my work which is that "Life can be easy". My teachers, Brandon Bays (The Journey) and Tolly Burkan always seemed to be talking about there being a choice about how life went. From that I developed the affirmation that "Life can be easy". It is a choice that we make. While we can't control the circumstances of life we can certainly control how we feel about it and how we react to it. How we react decides whether it is easy or hard.

Tolly Burkan seemed to have a different approach to life from most people, in the sense that while he was teaching fire walking what he was teaching had nothing to do with fire walking. It was much more about getting in touch with the spirit and living from a place of wholeness. It made my life very much easier.

I started this work very much in a place of "I can't". I've come 180 degrees now to where I know I can do things that I have really set my heart on. I figure out what I want to do and start taking the actions.

Initially the change was internal. It was a sense of belonging and of being worthy. My self-esteem and confidence increased by quite a large amount within a very short time. One of my beliefs is that before you can have a change of circumstances in the external, material, world you have to first change your inner world and that was the case with me: the outer circumstances did not change until there was change on the inside. Most people believe that you get confidence and self-esteem once you achieve outer success. I believe it is the other way around. You get outer success when you change your inner world.

In response to learning from my teachers my thought patterns changed. Instead of constantly buying into the negative thoughts I was having I started to decide which thoughts I'd accept and which I would release. The negative thoughts were still there but I wasn't listening to them as much as I had been doing. That allowed room for

141

some of the more positive thoughts to come out and I started to listen to them.

I started to take very small actions around my circumstances, nothing major at that point because I was still developing the confidence, just very tiny actions. I started to notice over a year or so that things were starting to move across much more quickly than I had envisaged. I became an avid reader in the field of personal development and wanted to find out what some of these other teachers were teaching. My actions were from this hunger to learn more. I went around reading a lot of books and listening to a lot of audiotapes, finding out as much as I could about how other people were becoming successful. I quickly realised that some of the greatest teachers were giving the same message in their own different ways.

By starting to have a choice in which thoughts I followed and which not to follow the negative ones started to fall away. Life did indeed become easier for me.

One part of my work is leading fire walks. Fire walking is a perfect metaphor for "Life can be easy". When you really start to look at fire walking it is one of those things in life which most people would think is impossible and yet is actually very easy. If you talked to people I have helped to do a fire walk most would say that in fact it was a much easier thing to do than they expected it to be. Hence I think it is a perfect metaphor. In life we think a lot of things are difficult because of thoughts we have around them rather than because they are truly difficult in themselves. The fire bit is part of the metaphor because so often we live life by standing on the side of the road watching the other people going past, wishing we were doing the same thing as they are and yet being afraid to do it because we might get it wrong. It is a perfect metaphor because on the fire walk you can stand at the coal bed and watch other people go, and yet still be afraid of getting burnt. Getting burnt is the same as failing in life. You can treat a fire walk just as you treat life, which is to stand there and watch other people do it with absolutely no intention of doing it yourself, or you can risk doing it, knowing that there is a small chance that you might get burnt. That to me is life. You can stand around watching or you can do something knowing that there is a chance of failure.

Many people arrive on my courses that include a fire walk with no intention of walking. At least 50% say they won't walk, but statistically well over 95% actually *do* walk the fire. These people are as surprised as anybody that this switch takes place because at the beginning of the day there was no way they would even stand next to the fire let alone try and walk on it. Ultimately that day is nothing to do with the firewalk. That day is the metaphor. Whether they walk or not the course is tailored so that they get something out of it. We take the firewalk out of it so it is not about the walking. It is about learning skills and techniques that can be used in life. It is no use learning skills and techniques on a course if you don't know whether they will work for you or not. So the whole idea of our trainings is to teach skills and techniques to allow people to understand the theory and to give them the opportunity to leave the course knowing that it works for them. They are more likely to continue to use the skills and techniques if they know they work for them, and that for me is the fire walk. Effectively, through the day, the fire walk is just an excuse to teach a load of things which normally people may not pay attention to. When people know there's a fire walk at the end they pay more attention.

It is about going beyond the books. Everything I teach now is available in books by the teachers who taught me. But the books are only the theory and what you absolutely have to do is put what they teach into practice. There's nothing to stop you just picking up a book and learning everything from it and putting it into practice. You can use the firewalk as an analogy even if you never go near a firewalk. I tell people that when they start standing in front of the fire it is almost as if they have got an invisible force field in front of them. It's like one of those force fields you see in sci-fi films and it is stopping them from moving forwards. In life when you have a sense that you can't do something it is as if you are right in front of a force field too. You have to move through it in order to do that thing which you fear doing. If you imagine the force field you can really start to look at why it is that you are not moving forward.

"What is it that is stopping you?"

The Teaching Of The Fire Walk Is In 3 Simple Steps

1. Pay attention
2. Prepare for the worst
3. Ask yourself whether you are prepared to take the risk

Pay attention. Pay attention to the feelings which are coming up in you, the pulls that are coming up, and notice whether you are coming from a sense of "I can" or "I can't". Straight away that is a benchmark. Now, if you find yourself in a place of "I can't" then the next question to ask is, "Okay, why do I have a sense of 'I can't'?" In the fire walk I teach two things which are taught to top athletes and to the astronauts who undergo NASA trainings. One is that you need to be prepared for the worst. "What is it that you are fearing?" You need to be prepared for that.

Prepare for the worst. Find out what it is that you really fear.

Once you have found that out ask yourself **"Am I willing to accept the risk that what I fear may come about?"** If you are then that is an opportunity to move forward. If you aren't then that is a choice you are making and effectively you are saying "No, I'm not willing to take this risk." In which case, just move on in life and don't worry about not going forward in that particular direction. You've decided that you just don't want to go forward in that way at that time. If you do want to go forward you know you are going to have to accept risk and you can start to focus on the best, because if you truly accept the risk then what you are saying is "I accept any possible consequences."

Then you can focus your entire mind on expecting the best without any of your energy being dissipated by the worst. At that point all you need to do is to figure out what actions you need to take in order to move forward. You're accepting the consequences which may occur. Now you need to know "What is it that I need to know in order to take the next step forward?" What you are looking at is not the big steps, "How can I achieve the goal quickly?", but at "What are the simple things that I can do right now which will take me in the direction of my goal?" These simple questions can be repeated again and again and that is what will take you towards your goal. Once you have decided on the actions the next step is simply to take the first action.

The further you go along this curve the more dramatic the changes that take place in your life and career will be and the successes will multiply. If people focus on what they can do today and that is all they do every single day they will be astounded at how quickly they get to their goal. You don't need to do a lot. You can do what you want to do within a fairly short space of time. What I say to people is "How big is your goal?" , "What is a realistic time frame?" And if they say five years I say "Okay, great. Are you willing to spend five years doing something each and every day?" If you are you can use this model. If you aren't you need to be a bit more realistic about what you want to achieve.

That is why: "Are you in a place of ' I can ' or ' I can't"?" is such a good question. It gets you clear about your motivation. What are the 'firewalks' you want to do in your life? Can you do them or can't you? And are you willing to take all the little steps on the longer 'firewalks' towards your big goals? With clarity about your answers to those questions life can indeed be easy.

About the Author

Sanjay Shah, Director and Co-founder of Prime Source, is one of the newly emerging breed of coaches – those who can go beyond the traditional models of coaching and elicit therapeutic interventions where needed.

This has given a significant advantage to Sanjay in that he is able to help his clients remove deeply held emotional blocks which in turn will help them significantly improve their performance both in work and in life.

Sanjay's focus is helping people to:

- Become self empowered
- Increase self awareness
- Remove emotional blocks that place a false ceiling on their abilities
- Live their life purpose

The practical effect of this focus is that his clients find they have:

- Significantly increased confidence and self esteem
- Reduced stress
- Finally let go of past issues
- Begun to live the life of their dreams

A Master Practitioner of NLP (Neuro Linguistic Programming), Hypnosis and Time Line therapy, an Executive Coach, Firewalk trainer, Reiki Master and Journey Therapist, Sanjay has studied with some of the world's leading experts in the field of emotional intelligence and rapid change. He is recognised as one of the leading Journey Therapists (www.thejourney.com) and Firewalk trainers in the UK and one of the few people to teach the work of Byron Katie (www.thework.org)

Sanjay's extensive experience in the fields listed above with his practical knowledge of human behaviour using the Enneagram have led to the Immediate Solutions Coaching Programme™. This unique blend of different disciplines has led to a thriving coaching practice with other therapists and coaches often being his clients.

Sanjay specialises in working with professionals who are dissatisfied with the quality of their results and wish to remove blocks that are in their way.

Learn more about Sanjay's work here: www.theprimesource.net

HOW WILL YOU LIVE YOUR MAGNIFICENCE?

BY TONY BURGESS

I strongly believe that everyone has magnificence within them, abundant and overflowing, making up the very essence of their inner core. Unfortunately, many people aren't yet 'living' their true magnificence. People often hide it from themselves and the world with the 'masks' they put on because they are afraid. Many people are rarely even aware of their true magnificent self. They may think their true self is not good enough, that it isn't acceptable. People who are not in touch with their true magnificence are often very much held back by beliefs about themselves. They may experience doubt about whether they have got the capacity to be magnificent in life. They may have had their certainty about their magnificence educated out of them and they may have been playing out their lives to other people's rules and values.

Although many people aren't yet truly living their magnificence, most will have experienced it as children in innocent, carefree play and achievement. In adulthood they will also experience moments of magnificence even when they are not really living it. These are the times when people let go of the 'masks' and really shine.

I'd like to share with you how I personally live my magnificence, how I locate it, acknowledge it, tap into it and let it flow.

Living magnificence is a personal thing and a great journey of discovery. Parts of the processes that I use may be useful for you to experiment with on your own exciting journey to 'living your magnificence' too. So play and discover and do more of whatever works!

Here is what works for me. Test it for yourself!

Visualise a magnificent moment when you were really feeling 'on top of the world', free and happy and flowing effortlessly. This might be a dramatic empowered moment, or a moment when you were really relaxed, you had let the 'masks' drop and allowed the real you to shine through freely, perhaps in a peaceful moment alone or maybe in the company of really good friends or a person who inspires you. It might be a time when you were very much 'in the flow' of an activity that seemed to be happening without thought or effort, almost as if the real 'magnificent you' had taken over. Examples of this would be in sport, writing, painting or delivering training, or in whatever else it is that you do where you experience being 'in the flow').

Be there now.

Experience it fully by noticing detail. What can you see, hear, feel, smell and taste? Notice what you notice with a sense of curiosity and play.

Where do those great feelings begin inside?

Notice the source from where those feelings are emerging.

Where are the beginnings of those feelings located?

Once you have acknowledged the location of the source of your magnificence, it becomes increasingly easy to notice it again and again.

For me, personally, it is pretty much just below where the heart is, in the top of my tummy.

I ask myself questions to get more in touch with this powerful source. What could it look like, how do I experience it and how would I like to experience it?

After a period of discovery I have now got a kind of double whammy of incredible experience. In one respect I experience it as an energy and light absolutely shining out into the world and touching people's lives and at the same time I experience it as an enormous powerful magnet attracting more energy and light and great outcomes in towards me. It has a circular motion to it (emotion in motion) and it is a powerful experience that fits my belief that "what goes around comes around". When I send good stuff out into the world, good stuff is attracted right back at me and I can feel this happening right from my core.

I like to experience my magnificent core more intensely sometimes. I deliberately spin it around inside, faster and faster and bigger and bigger. When it is spinning fast and full on I get such a strong and powerful sense that the magnificent core of me is both shining out and attracting in. This makes me feel very connected with the world in a really positive way!

Energy from other people will also 'power up' my spinning when I look out for their magnificence and connect with it. I also shine great stuff out to them as I tap into their energy. To connect with people at the level of magnificence, 'masks off' and totally genuine and congruent is a magical experience. When I look for the magnificence in people I think to myself, "Wow!"

When I see people smiling and laughing and being amazing I think 'Wow! I'll tap into that!' and use it to power up my spinning. Even if I see people who on the surface are doing angry, upset, scared or moody, I think "Wow! That is powerful, there is a lot of energy available there to be converted - I'll have some of that' and again I imagine tapping into their energy, I literally feel a surge of it coming from them (like electricity can arc from its source) and I use that to power up my spinning - converting it to a more positive energy as it spins. Then I use that more powerful spinning to send something great out their way – I shine love and positive intention and resources and magic right back at them – I can feel it pouring out towards them and connecting with them.

I haven't always done this spinning process. Richard Bandler (one of the co-creators of NLP – Neuro Linguistic Programming) introduced it at a training session I attended a number of years ago, where it was being used as a very effective tool for rapidly 'undoing' feelings of fear. Basically, you notice where the feeling of fear begins, spend a moment to consider which way it currently spins and then you can use your imagination to reverse the direction of spin which, because you have changed the structure, changes the experience; the fear stops. It was also being used as a way of intensifying amazing states by spinning them faster and bigger in the direction that was consistent with feeling great.

I played with the technique and now I use it mostly for developing my connection with and experience of my magnificence.

Another NLP technique that helps me to easily tap into my magnificence is 'anchoring'. Anchoring is basically associating a neutral action with an intense experience repeatedly so that very soon the chosen action actually triggers the intense experience. My chosen 'anchor' is to press my finger and thumb together on my left hand when I am experiencing 'being magnificent'. I've always got my finger and thumb with me so it is easy and convenient to perform that simple action to 'store up' energy into this 'magnificence trigger'. When I do that I am basically saying "Yep! I'll have some of that for later!"

It is great to be able to use my anchor to trigger magnificence at will! And once it is triggered of course I get it spinning and shining and attracting at a level that suits me at that particular time.

I liken truly 'living' magnificence to what some sports people refer to as 'being in the zone' where performance seems perfect and flowing, effortless and unconsciously controlled, as if that part of us that knows everything has taken over for a while.

Another way of looking at it is imagining being on a scale of one to ten in terms of being free and fulfilled and on the last bit from 9 to 10 is where you are truly tapping into your magnificence fully. It feels qualitatively different to let go fully into your magnificence at 10 compared to the other increments from 1 through to 9 which I experience as 'a bit freer' and 'a bit more fulfilled' at each increment. A shift from 9 to 10 (as I have made sense of it on my scale) feels like a *huge* shift – a kind of total completeness as the final piece of the jigsaw falls into place exactly – giving the full picture for the first time. You will know it when you experience it! Experiencing that last increment on the scale is a revelation. It is like an awakening that you cannot ever return from. It is worth exploring and intending a discovery of this experience for yourself because it will change your life in such positive ways forever. It is kind of intangible to explain and yet so tangible when you are experiencing it.

I believe that tapping into your true magnificence is mainly about letting go of 'surface stuff' with real trust that your magnificence is there waiting to shine through and that you can be certain that magnificent outcomes are heading your way. There are steps that help me to 'let go' in this way and get into trust and certainty that whatever is heading my way is exactly right.

Included in the steps is a process of visualisation where I say things and ask things with real conviction. Sometimes I shout them in my head and sometimes out loud. Key components that make up this dialogue include: GRATITUDE for what I have and for what is coming my way, focus on BENEFITS TO OTHERS that will come from me growing as a person and attracting what I want (this allows me to know that I DESERVE great things), OPENING UP to RECEIVING and ATTRACTING what is heading my way, and CLAIMING outcomes with clarity knowing in that moment that it is a 'done deal' because it is in line with my values and is going to benefit others massively. This congruent claiming leads to a sense of TRUST AND CERTAINTY. I also focus on SHINING great stuff out into the world, knowing that WHAT GOES AROUND COMES AROUND.

So as an example I might close my eyes, relax and start with a clear outcome in mind, such as attracting ten new clients. My visualisation would have visual elements to it and sometimes sounds, movement and feelings too. I run this 'mind rehearsal' as I go through an internal (or external – shouted out loud) dialogue that may go something like this...

"THANK YOU for my MAGNIFICENCE and my ability to connect with magnificence all around me. THANK YOU for the ten new clients that are being attracted my way. I know that me getting these new clients will BENEFIT OTHERS in so many ways. It will benefit the clients themselves, my family, the charities I support, even people I have yet to meet. And because this outcome is benefiting the GREATER GOOD and is in line with my core values and identity I OPEN UP to receiving those outcomes, knowing that I DESERVE them. I CLAIM them right now knowing that they are inevitably headed my way because they serve the greater good and because they are in line with my values and identity and mission. I ATTRACT them from my magnificent core like a giant magnet and I also SHINE magnificence out into the world, creating magnificent outcomes for others. I know that the more magnificence I attract, the more I have to give and the more I give the more I will attract. So THANK YOU for those ten new clients that are inevitably heading my way."

You can experiment to find out what words help you to tap into your '10' where you feel totally empowered and free and connected and like you are really 'living' your true magnificent self. Remember to say things with conviction and heart-felt meaning.

Experiencing myself at the level of magnificence and seeing the magnificence in other people is a joy in itself. So many people are seeing limitations and faults in people. Can you imagine if people were going round in their workplace consciously (and then unconsciously as it became familiar) seeing the magnificence in other people? It would give a whole different context to going to work. I love to do that. When I seek the magnificence in people they respond to it and tend to be more magnificent, or rather, they let more of what's already there below the surface show. Then it is about magnificence meeting magnificence – imagine the power of collective magnificence at work and play!

To sum up, for me, living magnificence is about:

- Locating the source in me
- Finding ways to access it again quickly (such as through 'anchoring' it to a simple action)
- Learning ways to enhance the intensity (such as through spinning)
- Having clarity of purpose
- Incorporating a sense of contribution
- Letting go into trust
- Increasing conviction and certainty
- Connecting with others at their core

This is personal to me and I trust that elements of the process I go through to get in touch with my magnificent core may be useful to others in getting in touch with their own magnificent core.

What are you going to do with your magnificence? What is your clear intention and purpose? Here are some questions about magnificence that can be worth asking yourself and others in different situations:

- What if my magnificence can attract (specific desired outcome) easily, starting now?
- How might my magnificence shine through in such a way that I attract the right people into my life?
- What am I going to attract with the powerful magnet that is my magnificence?
- How am I experiencing gratitude for all that my magnificence is attracting?
- What is it that tells me I deserve to attract my dream outcomes?
- What are we going to achieve with our collective magnificence?

About the Author

Tony Burgess is a Director of the Academy of High Achievers.

Tony has a degree in Psychology, he is a qualified teacher, hypnotist, psychotherapist and Master Practitioner in NLP.

As an experienced trainer and coach, most of Tony's time is now spent designing, co-ordinating and delivering performance-enhancement programmes for people who are hungry for success. He has worked with business leaders, teams within organisations, educators, students, sports people and members of the public to help them to tap into and release the full potential of their personal resources, allowing them to attain whatever outcomes they set out to achieve and much more besides. Before becoming a founding Director of Academy of High Achievers, Tony ran his own successful coaching and training company.

Learn more at: www.aha-success.com

Contact Tony at: tburgess@aha-success.com

Judy Barber

If There Were a Miracle Tonight and In The Morning Everything Was Exactly As You'd Like It To Be, How Would You Know a Miracle Had Taken Place?

by Jamie Smart

The first 'personal development' course I ever attended started with the trainer saying, "You are capable of far more than you think you are. You have all the answers to all the questions you will ever ask, already inside you." I was highly sceptical, but said to myself, "Keep an open mind and test this yourself." In the time that followed I started to learn about the amazing power of the human mind and began to realise that we are all far more clever than we think.

One of the most amazing examples of this I ever heard came from the world of hypnotherapy. Milton Erickson (the world's greatest dead hypnotist) told the story of working with a client who was totally unable to solve a particular problem. Erickson guided the client into a trance and then invited him to imagine travelling forward in time, six months into the future, to a point where the problem no longer existed. He then asked the client to remind himself (at that future point in time) of how he had solved that former problem. When the client emerged from the trance he announced that he had the solution! The client's unconscious mind had generated the solution, even though the client had consciously claimed to be unable to solve the problem.

Free Your Creative Unconscious

The idea that you can know more than you think is the principle behind one of my favourite questions, The Miracle Question. The Miracle Question was developed by Steve de Shazer, a pioneer in the field of Brief Therapy, and is one of the most powerful ways there is to help people to create a vision of how they would like things to be. It can be equally effective whether used in a problem-solving mode or in

155

a more generative mode. The structure of the question (as I use it) is as follows:

"If there were a miracle tonight and when you woke up tomorrow everything [in this area of your life/work/business] was exactly as you'd like it to be, how would you know a miracle had occurred? What would you see, feel, hear, experience and believe that would let you know that a miracle had taken place?"

The idea of a miracle gives the incredibly creative unconscious mind the freedom to conceive of things being the way a person wants them to be. It allows the internal 'judging' mechanism to take a back seat — at least temporarily. When you ask this question people will often enter a trancelike state, generating internal images, sounds and feelings. Their answers will sometimes surprise them and they will often enter a highly relaxed state while describing their 'miracle'.

If you would like to use The Miracle Question with other people, it's important to have had your own personal experience of it first, so take a few minutes to do the 'Your Own Personal Miracle' exercise.

Your Own Personal Miracle	Time & space: 15 minutes without interruption	You will need: Paper and a pen

Choose an area of your life where you would like things to be different from the way they are now. It might be an area where you are experiencing difficulties, or it may be an area where things are already going well and you want them to be even better.

Once you've chosen the area, ask yourself the following question: "If there were a miracle tonight and when you woke up tomorrow everything [in this area of your life/work/ business] was exactly as you'd like it to be, how would you know a miracle had occurred? What would you see, feel, hear, experience and believe that would let you know that a miracle had taken place?"

Now write down the answers that come. Allow yourself to imagine looking around this area of your life, experiencing the post-miracle situation.

156

- What can you see that wasn't there before?
- If there are other people involved, how are they behaving towards you?
- What are people saying to you?
- How do you feel?
- What is the atmosphere like?
- What are you doing?
- What new behaviours and skills are you exhibiting?
- How do you think and feel about yourself?
- What does this 'post-miracle you' believe?
- What else can you see that lets you know things are different?

Really allow yourself to explore your miracle. One of the nice things about this approach is that it can allow you to imagine how you want things to be, without having to figure out how it is going to happen. This can allow you to access your unconscious creativity in a very real and practical way.

A Change In Perception

The word "miracle" often conjures up thoughts of the seemingly impossible, but one of the things that often surprise me is how 'tame' the miracles people usually ask for are. In response to the miracle question people often will say things like:

"I'd wake up feeling good."

"Everyone on my team would be working well together."

"I'd look in the mirror and see myself smiling."

"There would be a real buzz around the office."

"I'd enjoy doing exercise, and look in the mirror at a slim me."

These things may not seem miraculous; in fact they are entirely achievable using Neuro linguistic Programming, Life Coaching, and any number of other approaches when used by well-trained, highly-skilled professionals. But don't let the fact that they may be commonplace fool you into thinking they are not miraculous. For the individual involved a change in their own perception can be the greatest miracle imaginable.

Additional Areas For Exploration

This change in perception is often created by vividly imagining life as you would like it to be using The Miracle Question. In fact, sometimes just the process of asking the question creates a major shift in the way a person perceives themselves and their choices. It can be useful, however, to ask additional questions to help a person explore the ways in which they can allow themselves to go from where they are now to where they want to be. Here are a number of other areas worth considering:

- Is there any aspect of the miracle that does not seem perfect yet?
- If you could wave a magic wand, and improve any aspect of the miracle situation even further, what would you change?
- How would the miracle affect your family and friends?
- How would the miracle affect your work situation?
- What are the benefits of not having the miracle?
- What would you have to let go of to make space for the miracle to arrive?
- What would be going on a month after the miracle? Three months? A year?
- What has stopped you in the past from experiencing this situation in your life?
- How can you start to allow that miracle situation to come into your life?
- What steps could you take to start moving towards the miracle?

Where Can I Use This?

There are numerous situations where The Miracle Question can be an incredibly powerful tool, including life coaching, executive coaching, therapeutic interventions, business visioning, sales, problem-solving, and many more:

Life Coaching

The Miracle Question is a fantastic way of helping a client to create a vision for the life they desire. It's also great for clients who say they don't know what they want.

Therapeutic Interventions

The question works well with clients who have difficulty imagining themselves no longer having the issue or problem they currently face.

Executive Coaching

It's great for clients who are 'intensely practical', and are resistant to exploring any goal that they do not yet know how to achieve. It's also great for clients who claim that they can't visualise.

Sales

The question is superb for getting a client to explore their desired outcome (rather than 'the problem') and feel the great feelings associated with it.

Business Visioning

It's a great way of getting a group of people to come up with a shared vision for their team, department or company.

Problem-solving

The Miracle Question is very powerful for helping people to shift from focusing on the problem to focusing on the solution.

Leadership

Nowhere is there a greater need for positive visions of the future than in leadership. Leaders of businesses, organizations, communities and countries have enormous influence over where their constituents focus. If leaders focus on what they don't want (e.g. dissatisfaction, losses, drugs and terrorism), those are likely to increase (if you doubt this, investigate the effect 'the war on drugs' had on US drug consumption). On the other hand, if they ask The Miracle Question and create visions of a world everyone would choose to live in, the effect will be incredibly positive and powerful.

I use the question indiscriminately across all the areas mentioned above. As long as you are comfortable and congruent when asking the question, your client will almost invariably be willing to answer it.

How Does This Work?

The Miracle Question takes advantage of a number of aspects of human consciousness and the unconscious mind:

What we focus on increases. The human nervous system is goal-seeking. Whether you're driving to work, pouring a glass of water, planning a business strategy or scratching your head, your nervous system automatically sets countless goals and then tests to see if they've been achieved. Over a period of time, we tend to move towards what we think about, so thinking thoughts of how you want things to be is a powerful way to start bringing them into your reality.

The unconscious mind is creative. When people say they can't do something, or that they don't know what they want, the mind goes "Well, if I can't do it, then let's not waste any time on it." On the other hand, as soon as the mind is opened to a possibility, by using The Miracle Question for example, the creative unconscious immediately starts thinking of the ways in which that 'goal' can be achieved. If you say "I can't do it", the mind shuts off. If you ask "How can I do it?" the mind starts creating.

People make the best choice they perceive as being available. For many people, being in a 'stuck' state is the best they've been able to imagine. The Miracle Question opens up another level of choices for them.

The unconscious deals directly with negation. Negatives are not processed by the nervous system in the same way that they are linguistically. For example, the command: "Don't think of a purple hippopotamus" is very difficult to obey. It is therefore most effective to state any desired outcome or direction in the positive. Focusing on how you *don't* want things to be will move you *towards* what you don't want. Focusing on how you *want* things to be has the opposite, and more beneficial, effect.

I've used this approach with numerous individuals and groups, from writers to sportspeople, from sales teams to boards of directors. It always has a powerful impact. But don't just take my word for it. Do it yourself, then use it with other people. You will be amazed at what is possible!

Free Bonus Question

Sometimes when I ask The Miracle Question, the client will say "I don't know." When that happens, I will often say something like this:

"Oh, I know. It's kind of a strange question, isn't it? But if you did know, what would your answer be?"

Amazingly, people will almost always give you a coherent answer when you ask this question. This is based on similar logic to The Miracle Question; that people know a lot more than they think they do. It's a great question to use whenever people think they don't know the answer to any 'inner-directed' question.

About the Author

Jamie Smart came to the world of Neuro Linguistic Programming (NLP) from a career in IT, first as a computer programmer and then rising through the ranks to become a first-class Project Manager. Today, as Founder and Managing Director of Salad and now a highly respected author, trainer, executive coach and NLP specialist, his published work includes the market-leader for learning hypnotic language, Ericksonian Hypnosis Cards™. His weekly NLP Tips newsletter is read by over 10,000 coaches, managers, therapists and NLP-enthusiasts worldwide.

A highly skilled and experienced SNLP-accredited NLP trainer, taught by many of the best NLP specialists out there (some of them way out there!), Jamie believes his skill can only grow as he continues to learn from those he respects. Recognised for his unique skills, he passes on knowledge and experience in an intimate training setting and teaches with a blend of humour, compassion and wisdom that is exceptional in his field.

Jamie believes in giving a thorough grounding of the complete NLP skill set, so his NLP Practitioner and NLP Master Practitioner training programmes are each taught over the course of fifteen days - 5 modules of 3 days. With such a rich understanding of NLP, garnered from all his teachers, he believes it is only through intensive and thorough training that he can really pass on what he has learned.

A leading resource for development and coaching instruments, Salad offers a comprehensive range of materials for learning NLP, Persuasion & Influence, Intuition and General Wellbeing. Consumers of these products range from those in business and enterprise, to consultants, life coaches and the full spectrum of people looking to unlock the power of NLP in their lives. The fast growing range of Salad products, which includes books, programmes, CD, and games, is available at www.saladltd.co.uk

PART SIX: GETTING TO THE HEART OF THINGS

The link between these three chapters is that the writers invite taking a careful look at what is below the surface. With Debbie Jenkins the invitation is to question, again and again, our motives for doing something, in a way that is constructive from a business point of view and that can reveal common ground between people. Gerard O'Donovan invites us to consider the person who is asking the question and to go through layer after layer of answer. Jesvir Mahil invites us to look beyond normal planning times to consider what is of fundamental importance to us. In their own ways they all get to the heart of things.

Deep down, what is really important to you?

Judy Barber

SO WHAT?

BY DEBBIE JENKINS

This powerful question can be used to ramp up the emotional potency of your communication. You can use it to turn seemingly mundane facts and features into powerful motivating reasons why people should change their behaviour or simply change their mind.

It can be used to gain support, help an individual overcome a block, persuade people to consider your point of view or simply to sell an idea, service or product.

But before we get onto how you use this question let's first take a look at...

How We Sort Data (Chunking)

We, as humans, handle data and information in some specific and measurable ways. These distinctions will show you why certain questions are not only useful but essential for connecting emotionally with your fellow humans.

The three big distinctions are...

1. Chunking Up
2. Chunking Down
3. Chunking Laterally

Let's use, for the sake of example, a Gorilla as our starting word.

If I were to say, "A Gorilla is a type of what?"

You might say, Primate.

This is chunking up.

You could chunk up further...

...Primates are types of Mammals...

...Mammals are types of Animals...

...Animals are types of Life Forms...

If I were to say, "What else is like a Gorilla?"

You might say monkey, man, giraffe, baboon, dog or cat, etc as these all belong in the same category as Gorillas. They're all examples of mammals or animals.

This is chunking laterally.

If I were to say, "Describe a Gorilla." you might begin to say words like two arms, two legs, furry, big and likes bananas

This is chunking down.

So what has this got to do with communicating powerfully? Why am I telling you something that probably seems obvious?

It is because nearly every person who communicates today is great at chunking laterally and brilliant at chunking down when it comes to describing their cause, their argument or their ideas. But they nearly all miss chunking up, completely.

If you want to create an emotional connection then chunking up is essential. Effective communication is really about saying a lot with just one or two words. When you chunk up properly you can account for all the detail while making a memorable, emotional point that is easy to pass on.

If you need a list to describe what you do then your communication will lack power. If you can describe what you do for people or why people should take notice at the highest level with a choice sound bite or word then you'll truly have emotional potency.

So chunking up for the sake of communication means connecting with people at their highest level. This typically tends to be an emotional or 'root cause' level and the effect of hitting the right emotional buttons here works like magic in getting them interested, attentive and open to positive suggestion.

Now, I'd just like to bring your attention to the distinctions between...

Features, Advantages and Benefits

1) Features (chunk down)

Features describe the properties, facts, qualities and elements of your suggestion, product, cause or argument. These things are typically only important and relevant to you and lead to long lists, boring introductions, tedious text in brochures and uninspiring presentations.

2) Advantages (chunk laterally / comparison)

Advantages compare the properties, facts, qualities and elements of your solution with the properties, facts, qualities and elements of other solutions. These things are important when deciding between one or more alternatives but are dangerous because they pre-suppose that the other person should make a choice between your proposal and another when what you really want is for them to make a choice between proceeding with your proposed solution now or in the future.

3) Benefits (chunk up)

Benefits require a beneficiary.

Benefits require recipients such as clients, customers or people on the receiving end of charity/voluntary work. These people typically have a need or want that they'd like taken care of. A benefit describes the positive outcome to your recipient of going along with your advice.

All three elements are important in describing what you're doing but benefits are almost always the most important thing in describing what the other person will get. And what they will get is usually the most important thing to them.

Finally, here's how to...

Use "So What?"

"So what?" is a question that enables you to chunk in all sorts of directions.

Used in its purest form it asks people to search for more meaning to justify the example they've given. This often leads to them chunking up to a higher level. It can also be softened to achieve similar results...

- So what could that lead to?
- So what will that bring you?
- So what do you really want to achieve?
- So what are the consequences?
- So what will that mean?

...it can be used to chunk down...

- So what's important in a...?
- So what's involved in...?
- So what specifically do you want?

...and even laterally...

- So what else is like this?
- So in what other ways does that help me?
- So what else do you do?

Here are just a few applications...

Networking

If someone asks you what you do and you say something like, "I'm a coach", then the conversation typically leads nowhere. They might, quite naturally, be thinking to themselves, "So what?"

Unaware that the person you've just struck up a conversation with is thinking "So what?", you, your brochure, advert or website text will probably then go on to describe what's involved (chunking down - features) and attempt to differentiate yourself by telling people why you're different (chunking laterally - advantages) and so completely miss the answer to your customers real question which is, "So what's in it for me?"

If you communicate in features (and most people tend to) then I'm going to hazard a guess that you've got a list as long as your arm to describe what you do and what you're about. I also have a sneaking suspicion that you're never really sure what to leave out or keep in either.

Here's how to use "So what?" to talk less and say more...

By putting yourself in the position of the other person and asking "So What?" to a feature, then asking "So What?" to the resulting answer and then asking "So What?" to that answer, and so on, you'll eventually chunk up to the juicy emotional benefit that the other person was really keen to hear all along.

Mediating

If you can chunk up beyond the detail then all sorts of opportunities for agreement, trust and rapport can develop. For instance, two children fighting over a particular toy might be focused right now on "getting the toy" but a little questioning will uncover that what they both really want at a higher level is to "have fun". Once you establish this common ground between the two then you have a strong basis for suggesting a solution, which might not even involve that toy at all.

This harmless example can be applied and has been applied successfully to all kinds of potentially volatile political deadlocks. If you can chunk up from the "We both want to own X" to "We both want to feel Y" then all kinds of opportunities will present themselves.

Here's how to use "So what?" to gain consensus...

By simply asking the people involved in a disagreement, "So what will having XYZ bring you?" you'll start to break down the resistance and attachment to the thing or point in question. You can keep on asking the same question, "So what will having XYZ bring you?" to the resulting answers until you (and possibly they) can see the common ground for agreement.

Helping/Persuading

Some people can get themselves in a real mess. They literally get 'down' into the detail of their current undesirable situation and have difficulty gaining any perspective... Using "So what?" can help you to illustrate the consequences (bad and good) of staying where you are.

Here's how to use "So what?" to create motivation:

By asking, "So what might happen if you don't sort this problem out now?" and continuing to ask, "So what might that lead to?" you will uncover some pretty nasty consequences of remaining stuck. To balance this out you could focus on the positive by asking: "So what will it mean to sort this problem out once and for all?" and then following up the answers with: "So what will that mean?"

Creating Media To Change Minds

If you do the work of chunking up before opening your mouth in a sales presentation or before writing that letter asking for support then you'll be able to start off a lot more powerfully. This particular approach requires forward planning and a little bit of role playing. It can be used to communicate clearly what it is your project, business or proposal will do for the people you're hoping to persuade.

Here's How to use "So what?" to persuade:

Now imagine, if you will, for a moment your business/project...

...Think of a solution, service or product you provide...

...How do you currently describe it to potential customers/supporters?...

...Okay, now put yourself in the position of one of these people and ask yourself, "So what does that mean to me?"...

...You should be able to elaborate on your initial description to provide more specific and relevant information about your offer...

...Put yourself their shoes again and ask, "So what does that mean to me?" in response to your elaboration...

...Aim to keep this dialogue going until you run out of answers to the "So what?" question...

...If you write these responses down from the bottom of a page upwards you will begin to see a hierarchy of benefits leading from what is usually a simple feature...

...The final response will often describe the core benefit to other people although the journey on the way to this will uncover lots of other useful benefits to consider and use too...

Next time you sit down to write start at the top of this hierarchy (the end with the juicy benefits) and build your message around that. Remember, most people are persuaded by benefits not features.

Here's an example...

Example "So What?" Chain

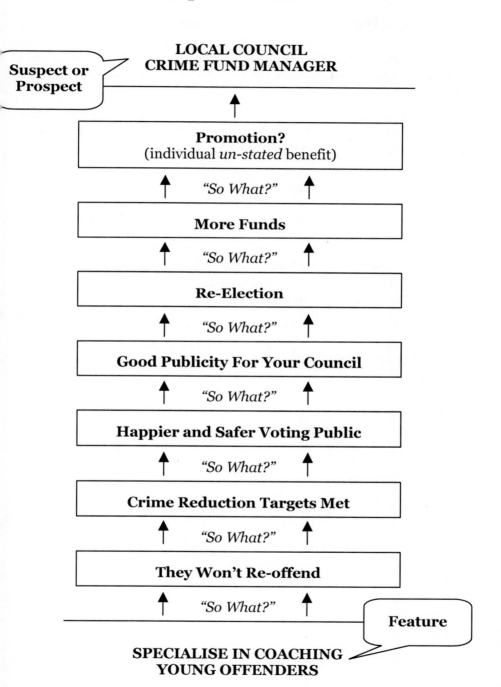

Taking a look at the example you can see that there is a chain leading from the feature/advantage at the bottom to a person/customer recipient/beneficiary at the top. Getting clear on *who* you're targeting with your message is crucially important. The more clear you are the better.

So that's it. A simple question with many powerful uses. See how you can use it over the coming days to improve the responses you get from friends, colleagues, clients and strangers. It's simple!

About the Author

"Dangerous" Debbie Jenkins is a best selling author, acclaimed speaker and serial entrepreneur who has launched 6 business and written 11 books on getting more success by doing and spending less since 1997. As well as founding Lean Marketing Press, a company dedicated to bringing you books by people who've done what they're talking about Debbie is the co-founder of BookShaker.com

She left her home-city of Birmingham, England in 2005, to wander the hills, woods and olive groves surrounding her cave-house in the south of Spain where she lives with her husband Marcus and 2 mischievous dogs, Dani and Fuggles

Find out more at these websites:
www.DebbieJenkins.com
www.BookShaker.com
www.Lamurta.com
www.LeanMarketing.co.uk

WHO AM I?

BY GERARD O'DONOVAN

Having been a coach for many years, in addition to having been involved in the training of at least 1400 coaches worldwide, I have come to the conclusion that one of the greatest skills that we, as coaches, possess and need to perfect is the 'art of the question'. In fact, one could say that another definition of a coach is Master Questioner.

It is important to remember that the quality of our life is determined by the quality of questions we ask ourselves. Some people ask themselves very mediocre questions indeed. For example, "What time shall we go down to the pub?" Others look at someone who has achieved great things and ask themselves: "Why not me?" It is similar to the difference between, "I can't afford it" and "How can I afford it?"

As coaches we have two responsibilities towards our client. The first is to provide them with a first-class coaching experience through the effective use of questioning skills. The second is to educate them in the techniques and benefits of self-questioning, helping them to realise the importance of regularly asking key questions.

Of course when it comes to asking questions we can get very sophisticated and clever indeed. We can use questions with suppositions and presuppositions. We can use open and closed questions. We can get involved in nested loops. We can use hidden questions. In fact we can make ourselves feel and look very clever using questions.

However I learned a long time ago the importance of simplicity and it is my opinion that the greatest coaching question of all is, *"Who am I?"*

This question is very often ignored. Why? Because it is easy to ignore; it can take us on an uncomfortable journey and one we might prefer to avoid. And yet it is essential if we wish to understand our core, the real person, the immutable, incorruptible and authentic 'me'. The 'me' we are really meant to be.

This question is the one that helps people come to a deep and satisfying realisation of who they really are. So this is one of the key questions that we must teach our clients to ask of themselves on a regular basis. "Who am I?" Again and again.

True happiness and fulfilment in life is only achieved when our actions and goals are congruent with our core values. Yet the sad truth is, most of us do not really know what our core values are. Unfortunately we take on board the values of others, the values that are impressed upon us by the media that constantly bombards us, and the values of the people we work with and the companies we work for. It is rare that the values we attach to ourselves are our true values. The inner conflict that this creates is one of the underlying causes for the level of unhappiness and depression in today's society.

You see, our values are in fact the mirror of who we really are, yet few of us look deep enough into the mirror to see the truth. Many thousand years ago there was a word written above a doorway in ancient Greece. The word was "Knosti" and it was written above the doorway of the Delphic Oracle. It is as true today as it ever was those thousands of years ago. It simply means "know thyself".

There is an old adage that says that if you don't know where you're coming from then you don't know where you're going. The same is true here, if you don't know who you really are then how can you possibly know what you really want out of life? If you don't know who you really are then how can you know what is truly important and how do you know where you are headed? I learned a long time ago that most people don't really know what they want in life, but are still prepared to go through hell to get it!

Being able to answer the question "Who am I?" with clarity and honesty will start the process that will make a profound change in the direction your life takes. This in turn will affect those close to you; your family, your friends, and your work. The way to make a real change in the world today is simply to do it one person – one mind – at a time. Start with the person who is closest to you – yourself of course!

How Do I Ask The Question?

It is important that when we ask ourselves the question, "Who am I?" we allow time for the answers to come. The truth may have to percolate up through a number of layers, and this takes time. You may have to ask yourself this question a number of times. For example, you may ask, "Who am I?" and the answer may come back "I am a teacher", "I am an electrician", "I am a solicitor" etc. The truth is that you are none of these things. You see you are not what you do...You are far more than that.

So when you ask yourself the question: "Who am I?" and you get an answer, you may then need to ask again: "And who else am I?" And again: "Who else am I?"

It is morally essential that we eventually find out who we are. So many of us wander through life in a kind of emotional and spiritual amnesia, deadening our response to life by producing images of ourselves that are far from the truth.

I recommend that when we engage in this important process that we do it in a place of solitude and stillness in order that we can be truly present for the answer. We cannot really experience anything without being present with it. True presence requires that we be attentive to what is happening in the here and now. It is our responsibility to be aware.

Exercise 1: 6 Months To Live

Imagine that you have just come back from a visit to your doctor where you have been informed that you have an incurable disease and only six months to live. However, during these 6 months you will be perfectly healthy, fit and active. Now write down what you would do, who you would see, where you would go and, very important, who you would spend your time with - and why. Would you change any aspect of your life right now? Would you continue to work in your job/career? If not, why not?

_____
_____
_____
_____
_____
_____
_____
_____
_____
_____
_____
_____
_____
_____
_____
_____
_____
_____
_____
_____
_____
_____
_____

This exercise should very clearly point you in the direction of what is important or even essential in your life. It is so easy to procrastinate but you need to attend to these things right now. It is obvious that these things are extremely important to you, so you should endeavour to achieve them as soon as possible – as a matter of urgency.

Exercise 2: Direction

This exercise will provide you with excellent pointers towards the direction in life in which you should be heading. It is important that you sit quietly with pen and paper, and write clear, specific answers to the following questions. Do not be influenced by others, or let negative thoughts distort your answers. Please give due time and consideration to this exercise: it is not uncommon for its completion to take several hours.

One...

Imagine that there are no barriers whatsoever to you achieving anything you want in life. What and where would you most want to be? Would you be President? An opera singer? Perhaps a great athlete or successful businessperson?

Two...

What in the past has given you the most satisfaction and pleasure?

Three...

The following list of words generally encompasses what we desire in our life. Write clearly your own definition of what each word means to YOU.

Wealth

Happiness

Health

Success

If you do not really know what it is you want in life, then how can you possibly achieve it? The answers you provide in this exercise will lie at the very heart of your final goal list. They will guide you towards what makes you happy and has true value in your life.

Who Am I At Work?

It amazes me when I see the leaders of major companies like BAT (British American Tobacco) being hailed by the business community worldwide as paragons, and real exemplars of how business should be run. Yet, there are tens of thousands of people dying every month around the world because of their product. Society is putting on pedestals men and women who create products that kill, purely for profit. I sometimes wonder if the inmates have taken over the asylum!

However, what price has been paid by these decision-making men and women?

Like so many others in similar scenarios being played out in corporations all around the world, these individuals are subjugating their own values for those of the company they work for. If only they would ask themselves "Who am I?" we might see a profound and radical change in the thinking of these leaders.

I have found that when I have worked with men and women in these positions and supported them in answering my question "Who are you?" I have enjoyed watching them travel slowly towards a true realisation of self. It is at this point that they have started to make a change – to really make a difference within their companies. Making and carrying out decisions that are based on power rather than force. Making a positive difference in the lives of the employees and thousands of customers of that corporation.

Much is said about corporate social responsibility: it is a phrase that is bandied about with gay abandon and sometimes solemness that belies the real truth, which is that most people follow and adopt the company culture, ethics, morals and values rather than expressing their own thoughts. This leads them to do things that are not congruent with their own core values.

Therefore there is a great need for all of us to get back in touch with our core values, because the truth is that in most of us these are highly commendable. It's just a case of getting back there and re-remembering who we are.

Do I Even Know Who I Am?

If we are not sure of who we are right now then how much more difficult it is to try and work out who we really want to be in the future. Especially as the media does such a fantastic job of indoctrinating us into believing what we really should be. From advertisements on television we know we should all be young, slim, good-looking, tanned, without spots or glasses. From numerous magazines we learn that by paying a lot more attention to ourselves and spending lots of our hard earned money (and in some cases, yet to be earned money) we can really make ourselves young, sexually desirable, good-looking, and successful.

The result of this is that we end up setting goals for ourselves that have actually been foisted on us. Not ones that are congruent with or even based on our own true core values.

In Conclusion

For many years I believed one of the greatest coaching questions of all was "What do you want?" This question can be asked in so many ways, you can come at it from so many angles and for several years I believed this was the question of questions.

However, long ago I realised that for some of the reasons stated above this is not the great question it ought to be because, as we have seen, we don't really know what we want at all.

I now know with a deep and profound sense of knowing, that there is a higher question, a more important question, a question that reaches deep down to the core. That question is "Who am I?"

You see coaching is about performing at your best through the individual and private assistance of someone who will challenge, stimulate and guide you to keep growing.

Essentially it is about helping you to reach self actualisation – a point at which you not only truly know yourself but within this knowledge possess a feeling of comfort with and understanding of the person you discover.

Coaching (or if we don't have a coach – self-coaching) is indispensable if we want to really reach our full potential, to be all that we can be, to truly reach a point of self transcendence.

About the Author

Gerard is the Founder and Principal of Noble Manhattan and his previous experience of many years in the armed forces has enabled him to apply discipline and thoroughness to developing his own business.

A renowned and widely enjoyed public speaker, Gerard talks not only of 'text book' theories. While well educated in business philosophies, he maintains it is his practical, real-life experiences that give him the edge over 'never-done-it-myself' trainers. His view is that only true experience combined with educational material can provide the all round approach that enables you to truly relate to, and help, people and businesses solve their problems and improve their outlook.

Standing ovations demonstrate how effectively Gerard inspires his audiences with penetrating insight and practical wisdom acquired through years of active business development, corporate management, training and interpersonal communications.

His unique training style and insight into business building philosophies coupled with boundless energy, make him one of the best of a few professional consultants and peak performance coaches who have actually done it themselves.

Gerard specialises in helping people to achieve peak performance in everything they do. Although he covers a broad spectrum of topics he specialises in helping and coaching individuals and businesses using techniques incorporating accelerated learning skills. Goal achievement, stress management, time management and helping corporations to increase profits massively through increased sales and personal performance are some of his areas of work. His unique training and teaching have been proven again and again to make a lasting difference. With corporations and individuals, Gerard's mission is simple – he will be your guide on your quest to be all that you can be.

Gerard O'Donovan's skills have been recognised by the Prince's Youth Business Trust, started by Prince Charles. He is also the CEO of the European Coaching Institute

Learn more about Gerard and his work here:

www.noble-manhattan.com

HOW DOES TODAY FIT IN WITH YOUR FOREVER PLANS?

BY JESVIR MAHIL

"Forever is not far away. Forever is right here and now; this instant is Forever"

My consciousness shifted as I realised that entering the dimension of 'Forever' was perhaps the same as entering the dimension of 'Now'.

When we are in the state of 'now', there is no past, present or future. Being in a state of timeless presence is like being in a state of 'Forever'.

When lovers meet and create their 'magic moments' of timeless love and a 'oneness' with each other that transcends the boundaries of space, they are in a space of 'forever' or 'eternity' or a kind of pure presence in the here and now if you like.

"How do our 'Forever Plans' differ from our long-term plans?" I asked. Is it merely that the latter are based on time whereas 'Forever' is timeless?

How can we have plans that are timeless? How can we go on journeys beyond time and space?

I started to ask my friends my cool new 'coaching question':

How does today fit in with your Forever Plans?

My friend John, familiar with the island of Bali, remarked that if someone gets married on the island, the Balinese believe they are married 'Forever'. Not just 'till death do us part'. No, they are married 'Forever'. He explained that a famous Western Feng Shui consultant was reluctant to marry her Balinese husband according to the Balinese traditional ceremony, as she wasn't sure if she wanted to be tied to this man 'Forever'. Interesting concept – I thought.

People aren't usually asked to make a choice between whether they want to be married to someone 'till death do us part' or 'Forever'.

Here we get into the field of religious beliefs and I realised that I was taking it for granted that everyone believes in the concept of immortality of the soul and that the physical body is shed and replaced just like the leaves on trees in a continual cycle of birth and death. It dawned on me that my question about 'Forever Plans' would be inappropriate for people who believe solely in linear time and in the ideology that there is no life after death; that our lives are finite, temporal creations that will blow away as ashes and dust into a void of emptiness when our bodies go past their 'expiry date'.

In India, when someone dies, it is said that they have 'expired' which I suppose is an attempt at being scientifically unemotional about the matter. What happens to our 'Forever Plans' when our bodies have expired?

This brought me deeper into the essence of my question and I wondered if there was a mysterious space in our being where all our 'Forever Plans' are stored for eternity.

Where is this space where our deepest desires, intentions and 'Forever Plans' are stored?

How do the so-called Laws of Attraction work in manifesting our 'Forever Plans'? Is there a space of timeless creativity that we enter to apply the Laws of Attraction in order to manifest our 'Forever Plans' magically and miraculously? What happens to all those things that we desire that do not get manifested? Is it because they are not part of our 'Forever Plan'?

When clients tell me about the goals they want to achieve, I help them to discover the underlying motive behind their desires by asking questions such as:

What would _____ give you?

What would be the purpose of _____ in your life?

How would _____ serve you?

If the questions are asked in a space of total relaxation and calm, the core answer to these questions inevitably illustrates a deep underlying desire for the ultimate experience of oneness with the Universe. To feel the love of being at one and in peace with the Universe captures the essence of the 'Forever Plan'.

Perhaps the question of "How does today fit in with your Forever Plan?" could be rephrased as "How much are you investing in Love, Peace and Oneness with the Universe today?"

Investment in love and peace is surely a plan although love and peace are beyond the constraints of time and space. Love and peace permeate our very being at the inner and outer level and their essence must therefore permeate all our plans in the here and now and also forever.

As I asked more and more people the very same question:

"How does today fit in with your Forever Plans?" Instinctively, it seems, people talked about the love in their life. They talked about their families and their sense of connectedness with the world around them.

"I didn't even realise I had any Forever Plans" one of them told me "but looking around at my family and all the love I feel for them, I guess I do."

Whenever I asked the question, it always came back full circle to love, peace and the 'magic moments' created with our loved ones. Those magic moments that we feel are part of our 'Forever Plans' and will therefore last an eternity.

How often do you create 'Forever Moments' with your loved ones? And, how does today fit in with your Forever Plans?

In response to these questions, my Shaman friend Inti Cesar, e-mailed me from Cusco, the Inca capital of Peru, saying that 'Forever Plans' sounded like his 'commitment to a vision'... It is his 'commitment to a vision' that has kept his wife and family together for decades and seen them through the trials and tribulations of modern lifestyles which have caused so many families around us to fragment. In order to keep a family together, there needs to be a 'commitment to a vision' and obviously some fundamental questions need to be addressed, for example, "Whose vision?" and "How is this vision created?" and "How can we create a 'Forever Plan' based on a vision that we would be committed to forever?"

Another friend e-mailed to say that he would like to see his ancestors and other departed heroes in the dimension of 'Forever'. This reminded me that some people already do this on a daily basis. The 'psychics', 'mediums' and 'clairvoyants' seem to have skills in crossing the dimensions of time and space and I wondered how their 'Forever Plans' appeared compared with those of us striving to achieve our goals and to make enough money to be free... or at least to have the TIME to do whatever we like; whenever we like.

Is it really TIME that we need to do whatever we like; whenever we like? Or a 'Forever Plan' that takes us into the dimension of NOW in an instant?

Whereas Inti is a very spiritual person living high in the mountains of Peru, my friend Shailen is an earthy, carefree kind of soul, living life in the fast lane in London and I was interested to hear how his point of view about 'Forever Plans' might be different. I was struck by the similarity of wisdom displayed by both these friends from such diverse lifestyles and backgrounds when Shailen recounted his perceptions:

"So many of us have grand master plans to achieve certain material goals by a certain age in our lives: to be married by the age of thirty; to own a 3 bedroom house by the age of 40; to be making over £100,000 per annum by the age of 45 or whatever it is ... you can insert your own details ... I sometimes wonder, what happens when we cross off all our goals? What are we left with when all those timed SMART goals are erased? What are we left with?" he asked.

Shailen is a business man and yet he talked about the pricelessness of friendships and love.

It is a common belief nowadays, although the ancient Egyptians believed differently, that we cannot take our material possessions with us when we die. So what are the things that we *can* take with us? What can we take with us into the dimension of 'Forever?' Perhaps it is the very things we can take with us into the dimension of 'NOW'.

My friend Thomas Power is committed to a vision. I reckon he has a 'Forever Plan' to create millions of worldwide connections with "A friend in every city." That could take 'Forever' you might think! Yes, it might just take 'Forever' to manifest a vision of a world where every individual is connected and feels connected with every other soul. Who wants to be so connected? This question reminded me of people who get disconnected, cut off from and isolated from the people they once loved with no desire to reach out and form new connections to revitalise and replenish their channels of self-expression. I thought about struggles and wars where people would rather exterminate those that they cannot tolerate, accept or forgive rather than realise the deep connections which mean that destruction of the other results in annihilation of the self. So, I wondered how a Forever Plan to become not only connected with, but a *friend* of every other soul in the Universe would become manifest with a true commitment to the vision.

At this point I asked *myself* the question:

"How does today fit in with MY Forever Plan?"

And I decided to reach out today to at least one stranger who is a friend that I have not yet met! Every new friendship is like a river stream that, with enough water to fuel its journey, will eventually reach the Oceans where all streams seem to merge in a space of timelessness – 'Forever' and everything you thought you left behind is right there in front of you *Now*. A place where the past becomes the future and 'Now' becomes 'Forever'.

About the Author

Jesvir Mahil is an educator and professional leadership coach with over 20 years experience in the field of education, teaching international students in London, Spain, Italy and the USA.

For the past 15 years, she has been based in London where she works as a lecturer at one of its largest Further Education Colleges, the College of North West London. Here, she has worked closely with refugees from areas of conflict around the world, teaching basic survival skills and supporting those who have lost so much in their lives, to move forward with hope and optimism. Jesvir is a management and leadership trainer for the college's commercial training company Fusion Training (www.fusiontraining.ltd.uk), training BBC and Brent Council managers. In addition, she has been training highly educated, international professionals and business people in both real and virtual online forums as part of her own private practice as a personal leadership coach.

The University for Life (www.universityforlife.com) offers customised management and leadership training and coaching to organisations. This educational business is the result of Jesvir's active participation in the field of Personal Development since graduating with a BA Hons Degree in Psychology in 1982, an MBA in 1999, and her training with the Life Coaching Academy, with Dr Richard Bandler, Paul McKenna and Michael Breen and Life Mastery with Anthony Robbins amongst others. She is trained as a Master Practitioner in NLP (Neuro Linguistic Programming) and is a BlackStar life member of the international Ecademy Business Network. She has also established local business networking clubs in Ealing, London and Hawaii.

Jesvir Mahil can be contacted at her website:
www.universityforlife.com

© Jesvir Kaur Mahil Director, University for Life www.universityforlife.com

PART SEVEN: BIG QUESTIONS AND CHANGING THE WORLD

All the writers in this book were keen to contribute because they want to support people in making positive contributions to life, so that is a thread running through all of the chapters.

The writers in this group are approaching this quite directly. Jean Houston's positive contributions to life around the world are simply astounding, and point towards what is now possible for us each to achieve for humanity, and what is now becoming possible for humanity as a whole. Lisa Wynn shows us ways to identify what we personally can contribute. Chris Howe's experience in Africa exemplifies how much cultures can teach each other when we are ready to learn. Babu Shah brings some ease to possibilities of changing attitudes to material wealth, and that can increase hope.

What kinds of contribution would you love to make in life?

Judy Barber

WHAT DO YOU WANT TO DO TO MAKE A DIFFERENCE IN THIS TIME?

BY JEAN HOUSTON

I work with groups of people in different cultures around the world. I usually work with large groups, but in many ways it is the same as working one to one. Here are ideas and questions you can use in coaching and for yourself, and which may be useful in your seminars and trainings.

We are all aware of how the world is changing, of historical shifts. Perhaps it is us who have the most profound task in history, deciding whether we grow or die.

Some of my questions have to do with why you have chosen to be here in this most critical and interesting time of human history.

I use questions like these:

- What are the questions around at this historical moment?
- Where and to what does your compassionate heart respond?
- What qualities do you need to fulfil your role in the great here and now?
- What lures you towards what you can become?
- Where do you feel the shadows of a call to action falling on you?
- What do you want to do to make a difference in this time?
- What qualities and things do you need to learn to make this difference?

From how they answer you get a sense of whether people have a sense of the possible or whether they are just barely going on in a state of serial monotony.

WHAT DO I WANT FROM THE UNIVERSE?

Here's a simple process. Give out paper and ask people to divide it into three vertical columns. At the top of the left hand column they write: What do I want from the Universe? Have them write a stream of consciousness about what they want from the Universe. They talk about health, wealth, making a difference, seeing beyond their current situation into the larger story that's calling them or whatever it is.

For the second column you very slowly enunciate words they can't anticipate. What - does - the - Universe - want - from - me? They don't worry about where it's coming from but just write a stream of consciousness.

For the third column they write: What do the Universe and I want together?

It's very revealing what emerges. It's one way of getting at what is really there for them.

When Did You Feel Called And What Did You Do About It?

I talk about being 'called', the sense many people have that at some point life asks them to take on a task.

I start by asking people about their experience:

"When did you feel a sense of being called?"

"What did you do about it?"

Someone might say: "I felt called when suddenly I realised I had to be a teacher." It might be: "I felt called when I had to get out of a terrible marriage." Or "I knew that there was something waiting for me behind the door of the ordinary and the extraordinary." Another says: "I felt called when I began to feel a stirring of the soul I had never felt before."

What Kept You Back?

Then people can learn from what stopped them.

I work with stories such as Parcival, a story of a young man's journey to find the Holy Grail. He learned to ask the right questions. I might take the structures of the hero's journey, for example when Parcival did not ask the 'great question' about who the Holy Grail serves. I'll ask:

"How did you refuse the call?"

"What kept you back?"

It might be, "Well, I felt that I didn't know enough." or "I was a woman." or "I was not adequate for this task." or "It was just too much for me." As people share their experiences in groups they can learn about what still stops them.

What Made You Say Yes?

To explore what finally made people say yes to the 'call' I might ask:

- How did you wake up to your task?
- When did you say yes?
- What were the situations that caused you to say yes?
- Was it just getting out of entropy, getting yourself moving?
- Was it a new order of health?
- Was there a book that fell out of the shelves?

What Supported You?

I'll ask what help people have received:

- Was there a person who just happened to be there?
- Who were the appropriate allies who showed up?
- Was it a strange telephone call?
- Was it a new kind of friendship?

And I find people often report receiving help from somewhere, like an ally arriving.

What Guarded the Threshold?

Many people experience crossing over a threshold. At the threshold there might be some sense of a challenge or guardian who stops them, but when they get through they enter a realm where they have amplified power.

- What or who tried to stop you?
- Who was the dinosaur in the game?

- What was the monster within yourself?
- Was it habit?
- Was it conditioning?

Universal Patterns.

I find that there's a common sequence:

- Feeling 'called' to take action
- Refusing or ignoring the call
- Deciding to accept
- Moving forward only to be challenged in some way at a threshold
- And then finding one has new and increased power for taking action

It is such a common pattern that it seems to be a universal pattern in the human psyche. When people work with patterns like that and start to relate their own experience to them it's very powerful. Asking questions from those patterns is a superb coaching technique.

I think coaching is calling another into their fullness, telling them they have the opportunity to play a role in the greatest transition the world has ever seen. We are what I call the 'people of the parenthesis', the people in the brackets between how life has been in the past but not quite at the beginning of the new. It is the optimal time for coaches because they are the midwives of souls.

PREPARING OURSELVES FOR RESPONSIBILITY

Regardless of how unfulfilled our own lives seem and how meagre our self-esteem, we are called into greatness by the necessity of our age and have little choice but to say yes. Many people think this is impossible. We feel inadequate before the trauma of our little local lives and also the sheer flood of world-destroying problems that grow beyond our limitations.

This causes some people to withdraw. Some become workaholics, find numbing sources of addiction or spend hours staring at the television. It is serial monotony and the progressive dimming of the passion of their lives. But many, and these people you can reach through coaching – and I mean a significant number – are trying to understand a momentous opportunity. They feel that not only is it theirs but they feel a hound of heaven going 'ruff ruff ruff' at their feet. These people will determine whether humankind grows or dies. The coach calls people through their larger sensibilities. These are the kinds of question you can ask:

- How do we prepare ourselves for these times?
- How do we prepare ourselves for responsibility for the personal as well as the planetary process?
- What qualities of mind, body and spirit can overcome these limitations of everyday life?
- How do you go about preparing yourself to become a steward of the planet?
- How can we be filled with enough passion for the possible to partner one another through the greatest social transformation ever known?

They are good questions for people to discuss together.

LOOKING AT THE EARTH AND PLANETARY SOCIETY

I was very fortunate to work with an astronaut, the sixth man on the moon. I tried to get him to remember what he saw on the moon.

He said "Jean, it's not what we saw on the moon that was so important, it's what we saw coming back to <u>earth</u>."

It was the picture of the earth from outer space for the first time. So many of the earth's people were seeing our planet floating in space. It activated something very, very deep in the human spirit because suddenly we realized we belong to a much larger unity of life and peoples. After seeing that picture of home we began to cherish the whole planet, not just our particular part or nation.

This tends to activate people. That particular 'Blue Pearl' photograph is like a time release capsule. Wherever you are around the world, talking to people who are just newly out of tribal status in Africa or talking to presidents and premiers, it creates the same response. It awakens something deep in the human psyche.

That picture of the earth that has activated something so deep is running parallel on an agenda with the very fact that this century has within it the coming of a planetary society.

It heralds, I think, the end of ancient struggles and the breath of new ways of using our common humanity in its many cultures. It means, and this is where I come in, a gathering through the work that I do around the world with so many different cultures of people. It needs a gathering of the potentials of the whole human race and the particular genius of every culture if we are to survive our time.

It's not that different people have different potentials; it's that different geographies, climates and conditions tend to activate something within the human psyche. There's the potential of the Balinese to learn aesthetic processes very quickly. There's the potential of a particular tribe in West Africa to be able to solve problems exceptionally quickly, and the potentials of other people to do this or that.

HOW CAN LEARNING FROM ONE CULTURE BE APPLIED IN ANOTHER?

Variations on that question can be asked in many situations, such as education, healthcare, business, social welfare, personal growth and creativity. Challenges arising in one culture can often be met by applying strategies from another. It is well known that we are coded with potentials few of us have learnt to use, but in this time of whole person transition we can no longer afford to live as half-life versions ourselves. The complexity of our time requires a wiser and greater use of our capacities. So that is something you can do as an individual, see what learnings you can apply in your life. People from other cultures are people to learn from, human resources.

Here's an example of what is possible. In Bangladesh there was a very bad legacy of British missionary education. I helped train teachers to really look at multiple intelligences and to ask themselves what methods they could use from other cultures. They went in making art and music central to the curriculum. When children are able to dance, sing, enact and 'be' information and use their whole minds and their whole bodies then they do not fail. They cannot fail. What happened in Bangladesh is that this went on and became fifty thousand new schools based on use of the many intelligences, with art and music being central and critical to the children's success. That's how powerful a question *that* can be.

WHAT IS IN THE BASKET?

In my work I often help people find inspiring new stories. For example in Kenya I tried to find a story that would suit Kenya and the problems of Africa.

I told a Bantu story about the man who goes to milk his cows in the morning and is too late. Their udders are dry and he doesn't know what could have happened. Next morning they've been milked and the same on the third day.

On the fourth day he goes out very early and sees a star boat floating in the air. A ladder comes down. Star people come down and start happily milking the cows. He runs after them and they scoot up the ladder, but he catches the last one and pulls her down. She says, "alright, I'll stay with you, I'll even marry you. I love the taste of this milk, but you must promise never to look in this basket."

Things go very well. They have a very nice marriage and she's a hard worker.

One day when she's away in the field he comes in early and sees the basket. He wonders what's in it. He thinks it couldn't be much and decides to take a peek, thinking she'll never know. He opens it up and sees nothing there. Just then she comes back and says, "You've looked in my basket!" He says, "Yes you silly woman. There's nothing there. What were you hiding?" She says: "Husband, you really didn't see anything in the basket?" He says: "No, nothing." She says: "Well, then I have to leave." She takes the basket he saw nothing in and calls her star ship. It comes along, up she goes and away.

I told that one because those people had such problems about seeing the future for Africa. At the end of the seminar I opened the basket and asked them: "What was in the basket?" They told me all the things that were there. They saw the great capacities that were there for them in government, economics, finance, development, schools and health. From that grew all manner of projects which now continue with people working together in new ways. Now they see what's in the basket and have gained a passion for the possible, and a sense of hope. That's an example of using a story and an imaginative coaching question.

USING OUR WISDOM AND BEING
AVAILABLE TO OTHERS

It's possible for people to think, to feel and to know in new ways. We can become more creative and more imaginative. We can aspire to a much larger awareness, one that is much more finely equipped to deal with the challenges that we face. We can learn to make conscious use of the complex wisdom of the body. When we do this we are able to help ourselves and others to see a much larger story that we are part of, and to get out of this sense of being in an encapsulated bag of skin dragging around a dirty little ego. We are able to have orchestral experiences of ourselves, and to bring out evolutionary latencies in our bodies as instruments. Then we know that we are part of a seamless web of kinship and we don't get caught up in our small selves.

I show people that we are basically being rescaled to planetary proportions. As we become resonant and intimate with our own depths we become much more available to others than we ever thought possible.

Here are some possibilities to consider in your work with people:

- Helping people to recognise what they are called to do.
- Showing people they have an important part to play.
- Using questions to connect people with their passion for working in the world.
- Asking questions to learn from other cultures.
- Using inspiring stories in workshops and coaching.

About the Author

Hilary Clinton described Dr Jean Houston as 'a walking encyclopaedia, reciting poems, passages from great works of literature, historical facts and scientific data all in the same breath.'

In America her mind has been called "a national treasure". Her speciality is developing and applying multiple methods of increasing physical and mental skills, learning and creativity.

A scholar and researcher in human capacities and co-director of the Foundation for Mind Research, she founded the Mystery School, for cross-cultural mythic and spiritual studies.

Holding Ph.Ds in Religion and Psychology, she has received many awards and distinctions. A protégé of anthropologist Margaret Mead, she co-led seminars and workshops with mythologist Joseph Campbell relating ancient myths and modern societies.

She has written 20 books and presented at hundreds of conferences and educational and business organisations in over 100 countries. She works personally with leaders of such groups, heads of governmental and non-governmental agencies, assisting them in developing their human capacities in the light of social complexity, and in rethinking goals and agendas.

As Advisor to UNICEF in human and cultural development, she helped implement extensive educational and health programmes, primarily in Myanmar and Bangladesh.

She has directed courses in capacities development, cross-cultural myths and spiritual studies, and chaired academic and scientific convocations. Her work has seeded hundreds of teaching-learning communities around the world. She devised a not-for-profit organization, 'The Possible Society', encouraging creating new ways for working together to solve societal problems.

Dr. Houston's ability to inspire and invigorate enables her to convey her vision of the finest possible achievement of individual potential to people all over the world.

With the United Nations Development Programme she's creating Social Artistry programmes training leaders in many countries and with associates has created the International Institute for Social Artistry.

Find out more here: www.jeanhouston.org

IF THIS BUSINESS DIDN'T EXIST, WHAT WOULDN'T HAPPEN ON THE PLANET?

BY CHRIS HOWE

The quality of the answers that you stimulate is directly related to the quality of the questions that you ask, or at least that was some coaching that I got several years ago when I started to debrief experiential learning activities.

What I have learnt since then is that it is not just the quality, but the simplicity that matters. Simple questions elicit far deeper answers.

For example, as a consultant I often work with executive teams who want to drive the performance of their business forwards. What I realised over time however is that some of them don't truly know what their business really is!

Now I could choose, when I realise that this is one of their key issues, to slip into consultant language and ask them to explain the mission/purpose of their business or I could ask a simpler question instead, "If this business didn't exist, what wouldn't happen on the planet?"

Experience tells me that the latter stimulates far more energetic and entertaining debate than the former. Even though you hardly have to say another word all day you will be considered to have delivered great value.

And isn't that why you coach, to deliver great value, however you choose to assess that value?

One of the things that I find as I travel around the world is that far from being different, human beings from all cultures are very similar. I have yet to find a human being who does not wish to be thanked, listened to, smiled at and, perhaps most importantly, recognised for their contribution.

At heart, everyone wants to make some sort of contribution; the real problems start when people don't think that they do make a contribution, can't recognise what their contribution is or believe that their contribution does not justify their existence.

In large organisations this leads to disengagement (a problem that is costing a mere £37-38 billion per annum in the UK – Gallup) and in the allegedly civilised world this is leading to increasing rates of depression and suicide amongst teenagers.

Helping people discover "what they contribute" is perhaps the most valuable contribution that any coach can make for their client.

Of course I knew this intellectually several years ago but I never knew what to do with it until a couple of years ago when I rediscovered this knowledge in a very different way.

In 2001 I found myself lost in the North Kenyan bush. The story of how I got there is too long to tell here and would add little to this book, but suffice it to say that my goal was to discover why it was that penniless street children in some of Africa's largest cities had higher levels of pride and took much greater responsibility than their more affluent, secure and comfortable counterparts in the allegedly civilised world.

A dear friend and colleague, Anthony Willoughby, had offered to take me into the bush in search of the answer to my question and, for a variety of reasons, we found ourselves to be lost without any food and water.

Good fortune however shined upon us, and we were lucky enough to find a Maasai community who were very welcoming and invited us to live with them for several days, sharing their lives, culture, huts and food.

I learnt more in those few days about building and sustaining organisational cultures, teamwork, developing individuals, coaching and mentoring than I have in 15 years of 'traditional learning'!

The two most pertinent lessons with regard to coaching were understanding your unique contribution and the power of responsibility.

Understanding Your Unique Contribution

After some time, I was struck by the fact that everything seemed to get done with no fuss or drama and not once did I notice people going to the elders to ask what to do next.

After a little more time, I started to become even more curious and approached people to ask them, "What is your job?" They did not answer my question directly but instead responded by explaining their contribution to the community, usually in a single sentence.

For example, the women would respond by saying that their role was to "Ensure that the community had water and shelter", this may sound simple but in an environment where the nearest water may be up to 20 km away, it is anything but easy! Without water or shelter, life expectancy would be pretty short!

A warrior would tell me that his contribution was "To die before anyone else in the community". A warrior's role is to defend the cattle and the community and hence if anyone else were to die first, he would have failed. With this weight of responsibility on his shoulders, a warrior will do anything that he can to ensure that he defends the community well; hence he will learn numerous tracking, hunting and fighting skills as well as keeping himself in shape by 'dancing' every night. To us it is dancing, to them it is a carefully choreographed gym session.

The Chief Warrior will tell you that his role is "To ensure that our community has the best chief warrior possible", which means that from the day that he is appointed, not only does he start to look for his successor, but they must, by definition, be better than him and hence he is looking to constantly improve quality!

Finally, and perhaps the person who had the most impact on me, was a 4-year old girl. She was holding a goat kid that was just a few days old and when I asked her what she was doing she said, "I am looking after the future food of the community." When she had been given the goat earlier in the day she was told this, "In your arms is the future food of the community, tend it well and we will eat, let it die and we will starve."

This is not a young girl who when asked, "What have you been doing all day?" will sigh with boredom and say, "Oh just goat herding as usual!"

The Power of Responsibility

In all of these examples you will see that not only do people know what their contribution is, but each contribution comes with huge responsibility!

On my second day I had noted that their camels (which represented two thirds of their wealth) were being looked after by a girl of seven.

When I spoke to the elders and asked them how she had convinced them to trust her with their wealth they told me that she had probably shown an interest in the job at the age of four.

At that time she had been told that she could have the job as soon as she showed that she was responsible enough to be trusted with such a significant job. At that time they showed her what she would have to demonstrate in order to prove her responsibility, then told her who could coach her and who would test her.

I asked them if they continued to ensure that she was developing herself to which they laughed and said, "No, if she won't take responsibility for her own development, why would we trust her to take responsibility for two thirds of our assets?"

It took me several months to realise just how much I really learnt in those days. It was significantly more than I have ever learnt on a similar number of days of 'training' in my life, but it took me a further year to figure out *why* I had learnt so much!

I realised that at the time of meeting the Maasai, I was actually quite nervous and certainly uncomfortable. I wasn't scared but I certainly wasn't relaxed and I finally realised just how well attuned my senses were to everything that was going on around me. Since I was so sensitive to everything that was happening, I was actually *learning* from everything that was happening too!

...and so to your reason for reading this chapter, what questions can you ask to become even better at coaching?

The challenge of coaching is often dealing with the consequences of the questions that you ask, so ask with care. For example:

"If this business didn't exist, what wouldn't happen on the planet?" is a great question to ask a team of executives because even if they answer, "Nothing", you can then work with them to find a solution to their problem by developing a unique contribution.

"If you didn't exist, what wouldn't happen on the planet?" is only a great question to ask someone if you know that they will be able to answer in the positive. If they are suffering from a low sense of self-esteem, this could be a positively dangerous question to ask and I for one am not qualified to deal with the potential consequences in that situation.

"If this role didn't exist, what wouldn't happen on the planet?" is perhaps a more helpful question since it takes the focus away from the individual and puts it onto the contribution that their role can make.

This does not only have to apply to a business context. If you ask any individual what roles they perform in life, they can always find some such as; Mother, Father, Son, Daughter, Friend, Breadwinner or Carer etc.

When coaching individuals, I do find it important to ask this question early on because it gives me several pieces of input as a coach:

- It shows someone what they are doing or could be doing that could be a source of pride and hence motivation.
- It often helps them to understand for the first time, the full potential of the role.
- It gives us an opportunity to explore areas of the role that could be performed even better.
- It helps them to look at how they might want to move forwards.

So Where Would You Go Next?

Well, it depends on what someone wants from you in coaching. I have clients who have found this one question so helpful to them that they needed nothing more to move forwards on their own.

If they want more help then there are other questions that have worked well for me...

"If you were to observe someone doing your role even better than you, what would they be doing differently from you?" The point about this question is that it not only suggests that they are already doing a good job but it deliberately uses a third party to review what could change. This is much more helpful than, "What could you do differently?" which in extreme cases triggers the response, "You're the coach, why don't you tell me?"

I have found that this unlocks things that really make a difference. One executive who I was coaching was avoiding facing a particular issue with their team and when asked that question, followed by, "and how would they do that?" they not only identified what they were not doing but also decided what they *would* do to tackle the issue.

If people are still struggling to move forwards or believe that they are not empowered my favourite question is, "And what are you prepared to take responsibility for in order to achieve that?" This is one of my favourite questions because nine times out ten the answer is, "My own actions and the possibility of failing."

If someone is really looking to change, try, "In an ideal world what wouldn't happen on the planet if your new role didn't exist?" followed of course by, "And what are you prepared to do to make that happen?"

Summary

So, what questions can you ask to help someone understand their unique contribution? How can you make sure they remain responsible for their own development and don't allow you to take that responsibility away from them in an unhelpful way? What can you ask to make them sufficiently uncomfortable to be more attuned to their senses and what can you ask to bring about pride, responsibility and focus?

About the Author

Inspirational presenter to conferences, sensitive facilitator of smaller groups and experienced business consultant. Chris prefers to be known as a change-maker.

Chris started his career with 9 years at IBM, in a variety of sales and sales management positions and then 2 years with Salomon Brothers, a major Wall Street Investment Bank, where he helped them to restructure and reorganise their business to face the dramatic changes that impacted financial markets in the latter half of the 1980's.

In 1989 Chris started his own business to take advantage of his experience and help a wider variety of companies adapt to a rapidly changing and ever more competitive business environment.

Chris has a fundamental belief that business is simple: it is merely complicated by fear and ego!

Hence he sees it as part of his mission to strip out fear and ego from his clients' businesses in order that people can freely apply their talents to achieve more effective results for the business, their teams and themselves.

He works at all levels within an organisation, in these three roles:

1. As Consultant, Chris works with Boards of Directors and Leadership teams, helping them clarify the purpose, values and objectives of their organisation.

2. As Facilitator, Chris develops and delivers the programmes. Using Experiential and Discovery Learning, Chris allows participants to gather knowledge and skills for themselves, without trying to teach people 'how it should be!'

3. As a Presenter Chris works with audiences that vary in size from 30-1,000, using business games to underpin key learning messages or story telling to make simple but impactful points.

Preferring the job title Captain of Fun, Chris is quick to challenge the paradigms of organisations, but also 'walks the talk', enjoying German motor-bikes, performance cars, and rock and roll music.

Learn more about Chris here: www.changemakerweb.co.uk

WHAT ARE YOU 'THE ONE' FOR?

BY LISA WYNN

There is a phrase in the film 'Two Weeks Notice' where a once again beautifully transformed (she always plays the ugly duckling role) Sandra Bullock looks across the balcony at Hugh Grant and says, "I cannot believe how easy you are being on yourself!" This chapter is a chance to be less than easy on yourself – to dig deep into your resources and find out what you are 'The One For'.

Continuing the Hollywood theme, in 'The Matrix' Neo was 'The One', the One for freedom of the human race; freedom from the machines that held them captive and prevented them from knowing what real life was like.

But Neo was not 'The Only One' – Trinity, Morpheus and the gang were all working towards the same aim. But it was only when Neo really accepted himself as 'The One' and stepped into being the full power-full being that he was, that life got really difficult for the machines! When we step up to the plate and accept ourselves as amazing, we can start to access all of the resources we have – resources that are naturally present but usually dormant.

In some ways Neo had it easy – he was told *what* he was 'The One' for. That discovery is part of the journey for most of us and we will deal with this, but first it is important to understand the possible obstacles along the way.

"What are you The One for?" usually gets a blank face as a reply when asked cold like that. There are several enemies to this process and these are best addressed first. This work takes you way into your personal power so it's important to know now that your ego has a strongly vested interest in preventing you from doing this work.

The ego has a very efficient personal thermostat which maintains the status quo very effectively. Many – probably most – people wander through life doing their best in the moment. Being the best father, mother, daughter, employee, student, boss that they can be – or believe that they can be. You are already in a select but growing group of people who are questioning that – questioning what they know; what they are here for and what is really important to them in life.

And, without such questions there can only be small changes.

There are some questions that lead to huge personal growth – and huge growth for humanity. "What are you The One for?" is one of those questions.

Big questions get big results. They stretch the self image beyond its usual experience of life and more importantly beyond its experience of itself.

Big questions take you out of who you currently are and into the realm of possibilities and limitlessness, allowing you to dance well outside of the self image. Although we return to it afterwards, the 'damage' is done – we have stretched the self image and are now bigger than before; more able to imagine a greater realm of possibility and better able to conceive of playing bigger in the world.

"What are you The One for?" is one of those questions that shifts the self image.

Major change at this level feels like an affront on your identity and the ego cannot have that! Some of the ruses it will try and use to keep you the same are:

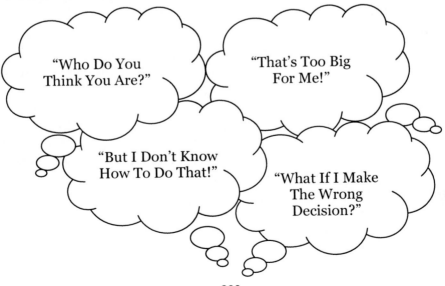

"Who Do You Think You Are?"

"That's Too Big For Me!"

"But I Don't Know How To Do That!"

"What If I Make The Wrong Decision?"

And so on. Just stay aware of such attempts to hold yourself small. Watch for them and just put them to one side for the duration of the exercise.

To put your mind at rest before you start, there are a few things that it is important to know:

This is not like "Life Purpose" work where it is traditionally held that you are born for one true purpose. Being 'The One' can change regularly. Maybe you are 'The One' for one thing this week and something different next week. It is about partnering with what wants to happen now and staying open to the fact that the Universe might have different plans for you in the future.

You might not be The Only One for a particular piece of work. This is about stepping up to the plate and really stepping into what wants to happen for the world and for humanity. It is not about being precious with your own role and it is not about having to do everything yourself. I have a client who has stepped into being 'The One' for Parental Respect. Is he the only one working towards this? Of course not. But he is thoroughly committed to this and is working to bring it to the world with every action he takes. Remember Neo was 'The One' but was working as a member of a team too.

Don't be distracted by the thought that you don't know the 'how to' element of being The One. The really good news is that once you have identified what you are 'The One' for, what wants to happen through you will start to present itself easily and clearly to you.

THE JOURNEY TO BEING THE ONE

Step 1: Access your potential

There are different levels of potential that we dance in and out of in our lives.

Personal potential: the potential to be, do and have all that we can.

Greater potential: the potential that we have to make a difference to others within our community, business, family, profession

Profound potential: the potential that we have to operate at a level that benefits humanity, changing the human consciousness to a different level and making life different from now on.

Most personal development works at the level of personal potential. We need to go deeper in order to change the world!

To access your profound potential, take a moment to still yourself. Close your eyes and inhale and exhale deeply and gently. As you breathe out feel your awareness of your body. Feel the breath and feel the chair or ground beneath you. Be fully aware of your body in this space.

Now, as you breathe out, take your awareness out beyond your body – keep breathing and as you do so, let your awareness grow with every out breath. Become aware of the whole room, then the whole building, the whole county ... become fully aware of the whole country ... continent and then planet.

Test your awareness. Check in with another country or part of the world. See the Taj Mahal or the tsunami-stricken shores of Sri Lanka. Bring your awareness to children playing in the local school or in an aid school in Africa.

Let your awareness focus in on where it wants to go and then back to the full planet.

As you do this really feel your awareness as being huge and global and then allow it to go way beyond global. Let your awareness be boundless, free of limitations and boundaries.

And just sit in that expansiveness. How does it feel to sit or stand in that amazing, huge expansion of awareness?

Enjoy it. Most people say it feels exciting, dynamic, calm, grace-full, creative ...

People often describe it as "tingly" or "buzzy".

However it feels to you, just sit and enjoy the sense of limitlessness. You are beginning to touch your profound potential.

Step 2: What do you want for the world?

If you had a magic wand and a single chance to wave it, which global issue would you address with that stroke? Capture your thoughts now:

If you were to 'cure' that issue, what would that bring to/mean for the world?

Step 3: What are you The One for?

This is a big jump and well worth working through with a coach. It is about really stepping up to the plate and owning your commitment to the last answer. Remember to let go of all of the limiting thoughts that may crop up.

First of all, just intend to know the answer. Intention is a powerful and underrated force for change.

Try the following questions to support this further. Answer the ones that resonate for you rather than feeling you have to answer them all.

What would you love people to say about you when you're not there to hear?

What would need to have happened for your life to feel well-spent?

What do people naturally come to you for already? (Personally and professionally)

What are you most passionate about?

What do you stand for?

Now ... what are you The One for?

Still struggling? Here is a client example. It is a rough transcript of a coaching call with an executive of a large multi-national company. We've already done the part of the exercise for expanding awareness:

Coach: What do you want for the world?

Client: A sense of order. Everything in its place and everyone fitting in and feeling great about themselves.

Coach: Wow. Sounds amazing. What would that bring to the world?

Client: Hmmmmm ... peace. A sense of deep harmony ... and joy.

Coach: Silence.

Client: And lightness. A sense of possibility and lightness.

Coach: How would that lightness show up in the world?

Client: Well, in the workplace people would treat each other with respect, love and honesty. We would trust each other and work as a team, still focussing on the bottom-line but achieving it through people not despite people.

Coach: Nice phrase. Love it. And what is the profound potential for the world in this way of being?

Client: Well, if we brought in that level of corporate culture, other companies would need to match that in order to keep their employees from coming to us. All companies would have to raise their game in terms of how they treat employees.

Coach: Fantastic. And what would that give to the world?

Client: People would go home from work fulfilled and happy, not angry and exhausted. Families would benefit and marriages would survive.

Coach: So, what are you The One for here?

Client: Long silence ... I am The One for Fulfilling, Profitable Workplaces.

Coach: Thank you.

Step 4: Aligning with being The One

Remember that I said it was not necessary to worry too early on about what you would do or how you would go about it? Well, neither of these are in the next step!

The next step is about really being The One – stepping into living as The One for whatever you have come up with. When you align with this, synchronicity kicks in and things start to happen that you could never have planned for. Yes, you will come up with 'how to' and plans and strategies as well, but don't push for them.

First learn to align with and enjoy the feeling of being The One.

Exercise:

1. Do the exercise to expand your awareness to beyond global.

2. Now from there, really breathe through the feeling of being The One. Sit in the feeling of being The One and become aware that the more you breathe through those feelings, the more they generate within you. The more you give them to the world, the more available they are to you.

3. Now, ask yourself: What do I need to do personally to align more closely with what I am the one for?

4. Open your eyes and capture your thoughts on paper.

One client told me she was The One for Play at Work; for really bringing a sense of wellbeing and fun to the corporate world. When she did the expansion exercise and asked herself the question above, she felt that she needed to have more fun in her own life – in and out of work but particularly out of work. She decided to make a list of friends she hadn't seen for ages or who really made her laugh and arrange some really fun-filled evening events.

Spend some time now listing the things that you could do in order to align yourself with the thing that you are the One for:

Now ... which one(s) will you start with? And when will you do them? What do you need to put in place to make sure they happen?

Take a few minutes now to answer those questions for each one you decide to put in place. Keep the list for future reference.

As well as doing things differently, I invite you to spend time *being* differently. Try expanding your awareness and then staying expanded whilst you make a call or walk to the canteen, or talk to a child. Feel for how the other person responds differently or for what you say or don't say.

Step 5: Watch for the signs

There isn't scope in this chapter to explore and develop this question in every direction possible, and this process is not designed to take the place of a coach working with you or your team or company on this work. A coach will help you to access this state of being and leverage it to create stunning action plans, lucrative business ideas and fabulous parenting skills – whatever you want for yourself and the world.

However, a very good fifth step is to stay alert! Watch for the signs that this is working.

- What is changing?
- How are people responding differently to you?
- How much happier are you?
- How many creative ideas are coming to you?
- How many new clients do you have?

Have fun and BE happy.

About the Author

Lisa Wynn is a Professional Certified Coach (ICF), an Accredited Master Coach (ECI) and a qualified Wealth Creation Coach. As well as being an entrepreneur, wife and mother, Lisa is also a sought after coach and speaker.

She has an international client base and works with individuals, businesses and corporations to create lucrative, fulfilling work and a bottomline that thrives through people development.

Lisa is The One for Fulfilling, Lucrative Work! Her passion is in enriching people's experience of life and work. She is Director of Membership (with responsibility for Professional Development) for the International Coach Federation and has been featured in the media on both sides of the Atlantic. She runs seminars internationally on 'Creating Prosperity' and 'Core Success for leaders'.

Learn more about Lisa and her work here:

www.corporatepotential.com / www.prosperitycoaching.com

Judy Barber

WHAT DO YOU THINK LIMITS THE WEALTH COMING INTO YOUR LIFE?

BY BABU SHAH

The biggest obstacle to people achieving their financial goals are their 'limiting beliefs'.

As you will most likely recognise, we take on beliefs from the moment we are born. Those who are fortunate enough to be born into and grow up in a wealthy environment find that they do not experience material lack in their lives, unlike those from a poor environment. As I write this chapter I am in South Africa, where most of the population would fall into the latter camp. My reason for being here is to help shift the balance by using some powerful questions to break down long-held social and global 'limiting beliefs' that hold back not only South Africa, but most of the developing world.

So how do we do this?

First, by gaining an understanding of wealth and money, and redefining values – we measure our wealth by our assets. Here is the list of assets in order of their value in the west:

- Amount of money [net worth]
- Material possessions
- Physical looks
- Health
- Happiness

In fact what is really valued most is happiness, and everything above is just a vehicle to achieve that feeling.

Because of western values and the power of global television and advertising, people in 'developing countries' are being programmed to put these same values above happiness. People in these countries started out living close to nature, finding happiness in the smallest of things, sitting by a river, socialising and so on, and their need for money was far less significant than it is today.

Money corrupts the creative spirit which should be able to find unique and ingenious solutions to our wants and desires – you only have to go to, say, India to see how the 'rubbish' that we throw away is recycled into all kinds of useful objects.

Take for example a man in the west who has just lost his job. He may feel as if he has lost his worth too: he may even feel that life as he knew it has ended. If you could only get that person to stop looking at the world through their 'money values', something strange and wonderful would occur. Reality comes flooding in, and the person becomes free from the hypnosis of money being the key to happiness.

What does that mean, "reality comes flooding in"?

Well, you might be aware that whatever you focus on, you experience. If your mind is filled with thoughts, worries and insecurities, then you will miss many of the opportunities that could be right in front of you. Sometimes a person becomes so 'down' that they feel that there are no more options left for them, and they are ready to give up. What happens mentally at that point is that the conscious mind, or thinking mind, stops wandering. At this point we literally 'get out of our minds' and begin really experiencing life; and reality comes flooding in.

A person facing death would experience something like this. In fact a heightened awareness has been reported by countless people who have had near death experiences.

Those people, who live in the so called third world, generally have minds that are less cluttered than their western counterparts. They have an ability to experience their environment at a level of detail that most of us could not imagine – they seem to predict impending disasters that we in the west still cannot predict with all our technology.

Getting back to our man who has just lost his job, how does a person who has dropped their material values and gained happiness also get material possessions, and in abundance? The answer has been around for as long as life has been on the planet, and I quote from the Bible: "Seek ye first the kingdom of God, and everything else will be bestowed upon you". The people in developing countries may never have seen a bible, but they are generally happy, have everything they need, and have abundance, when we don't use our 'possession-based' values to measure their success.

Happiness is energy. Everyone wants it, and those who have it attract more of it: they also attract opportunities to them in greater abundance than those who do not have this quality. It takes away the feeling of low self-worth, fear, doubt, worry and anxiety. and gives the person strength and courage to take on new challenges and opportunities.

I have coached hundreds of people to let go of their problems by just experiencing happiness. The results have been tremendous. One man, whose accountant was telling him that he owed £40,000, was later informed by the Inland Revenue, that they instead owed *him* money and *gave* him an £80,000 rebate! Let's break down the detail of how this (and countless other examples of this) took place, in a way that anyone reading this can experience for themselves.

I got a call from Fred requesting my help. I explained to him the nature of thoughts, about how whatever he was thinking was going on in his life was not necessarily real, and how if he could entertain that possibility then there was an opportunity for a positive change.

Fred agreed, so I explained that what we now needed was to interrupt his train of (negative) thoughts. We agreed that anytime that he told me about his problem, I would ask him about the weather, and he must answer the question in detail. This conversation would continue with me asking about the weather repeatedly, until Fred had learnt that it was fruitless to keep going on about his problems. At this point, I asked Fred what he noticed around him. He started describing the objects around him, their colour, size, texture, the feelings he felt, warmth, a little draught, and how he was feeling curiously calm. He mentioned sounds he heard, as well as some pleasant smell, a perfume.

"Was all this detail there before?" I asked Fred. "I don't remember. I was too caught up in my worries" was his answer. "Do you realise how this solves your problem?" I asked Fred, "no" he replied. When you stop worrying about a problem, it ceases to exist as a problem, and this vacuum creates a space for a solution to enter. I kept him focused on describing in detail his immediate environment for the duration of our coaching session, and left him with homework to do before our next session which was to describe his local park. The next session I was greeted with, "You won't believe this, but..." and he told me about a miraculous answer to the problem. Fred had just learned that he was getting an £80,000 tax rebate!

In a typical coaching scenario, I would always start with a story similar to the above, that creates a bond of trust, and relaxes a person into knowing that there is an answer to their situation, and that you will be able to assist them. The next step is simple: offer them a choice. "Do you want to continue focusing on your problems, or do you want to be happy?" If they still insist on focusing on problems then you have not yet convinced them.

But that rarely happens when you yourself are convinced of this approach, and are a living example of it. So make sure you are! Assuming then that they choose happiness, then BINGO, you are 90% there.

Helping Someone To Change Their State

Here is a series of simple questions and steps that will help someone refocus, and change their state.

Get them to close their eyes to help focus even better:

"Can you think of a time when you felt really happy, and everything was going fantastically well?"

...yes?

"Can you describe it?"

"Can you me more about what you are seeing/feeling/hearing?"

"Is there a taste or smell?

"Fantastic! Intensify the feelings. See it bigger and brighter than ever before. Make the sounds louder than ever."

As they do so, encourage them with positive affirmations such as: "That's good", "You're doing great," and "That's amazing!" (say it with at least as much intensity as they have, and more, so that they take your lead).

Continue until you can see that the person is now in a happy state, and then ask:

"Now from this powerful and creative state, what could a person who has (describe their problem) do?"

This helps them see the issue as an observer, and therefore to be more detached. It allows them to be more creative. Now help them to explore each solution, so that it is workable, get them to agree to some actions, and hold them accountable to keeping you informed of their progress by arranging further follow up calls. Make sure that on each call you begin by re-creating that happy feeling or experience.

I'd now like to share some of my own experiences of being able to turn around difficult financial situations, and I suppose my greatest advantage was that I had nothing to lose. Here is the first:

In my school days I really wasn't very good academically and I found myself repeating my final year because I had failed to get any of the basic qualifications of secondary education. I managed to get a place on an engineering apprenticeship which would have qualified me to maintain engineering machinery. Although I had little going for me, I fell head over heels in love with a girl who was smart, beautiful, and way out of my league. Being too simple to know that, I hung out where she would be, in a library on Saturday – studying! While I had no intention of doing the same, the fact that she seemed not to take interest in me, plus my stubbornness to be close to her led me to obtain not just one, but 2 university degrees. Why did this happen? Because your environment shapes your focus. I lost the old non-academic me.

By the way, I have been married to that girl for 18 years now, and also have enjoyed financially rewarding careers with Blue Chip companies, as well as starting and selling an international business in investments. Not bad for a school dropout.

My next example is from the early stages of my career with a telecom company. Having started with this organisation at the bottom of my profession, I was losing interest in my job and consequently my performance was suffering. I felt trapped: I was earning a reasonable salary, and the more poorly I performed the less confident I became in finding another position elsewhere. The company announced some voluntary redundancies and I decided to apply. I found that I was allowed to go more quickly than I had anticipated. Despite having no idea what opportunities were out there I stayed calm and confident. Within 3 days of being without work I was head hunted at a salary double that of my previous job.

Belief and trust in the unexpected happening allowed me to give up working before the age of 40, having had a successful private company. I now have time to share this key to successful living with others.

Here is a final piece of advice for anyone who might be inspired to live in this way. If you are looking for role models to learn from, like most people, you might think of looking at the most successful, like Donald Trump or Bill Gates. Instead, spend time observing children and ask yourself: "How do children get what they want?", "How do they react when things don't seem to go their way?", "Do they hold on to their failures?", "How often do they get their way?" The younger the child, the better the role model.

I wish you all the best in your lives.

About the Author

Babu Shah is an Educo Life Coach.

He started his career as a Design Engineer in 1987, having graduated with a 2:1 Hons. Degree in Engineering Technology.He then furthered his education with a Post-Graduate Diploma in Computers and Communications in 1989/1990, to then spend a further 8 years in the Telecoms industry working for Blue Chip companies such as Cable & Wireless, Racal, and Enterprise Oil. Babu started his training in Mind Technology in 1996, studying NLP (Neuro Linguistic Programming), meditation/yoga and Educo while continuing his IT-Technical Sales career. As a result of increasing confidence, and a more focused and trained mind he started his own business (TICN) in 1998. TICN was later franchised into 3 countries achieving revenues of over £1,000,000 in Ireland from start in 1 year. TICN became largest organisation worldwide in setting up private investment clubs.

Now Babu focuses on helping others to gain success using the Educo system (created by Dr. Tony Quinn, Dr of philosophy, Masters in clinical hypnosis, and NLP) that has university proven results in:

- Goal achievement: up by 67%
- Business revenue: 360% increase over 3 years
- Life Satisfaction: 55% increase over 5 years
- Finances: 88% a year, 264% over 3 years!
- Body sculpture: 3lb gain in muscle, and 8lb loss of fat, over 12 days

Contact Babu at: shahbabu@hotmail.com

Judy Barber

PART EIGHT: ALLOWING FOR, FINDING AND CREATING QUESTIONS

To give the book an open ending, these chapters consider further possibilities of coaching questions in creating change. So in a sense they lead on from what has been raised earlier in the book towards empowering people to have creative conversations that allow for future development. Aboodi Shabi asks a question about allowing space for something new in a conversation. Lourdes Callen considers the questions people have, individually, in groups and as humanity, and the importance of working with one's own questions. Mine is about encouraging people to ask questions, about different kinds of questions , using questions and creating questions.

What are your questions?

Judy Barber

WHAT WANTS TO MANIFEST?

BY ABOODI SHABI

"What wants to manifest?" is the question that I keep in the background when I am coaching, and which informs and creates the mood of my approach to coaching.

One of the things it does is to stop me intervening to try to fix things for someone. It lets me leave a lot of space for the client. It really reminds me that there is nothing to do but to listen and create space.

As human beings, and even as coaches, we live in a world where we usually tend to attempt to find solutions to our dilemmas (and the dilemmas of others), or to leap in, in some way.

Asking "What wants to manifest?" helps me to be okay with the discomfort of hanging out in the space where someone has room to reflect more. In that space there is the potential for unfolding something they didn't know was there – and I *certainly* didn't know was there.

How do we as coaches, and in life, create that space? Simply put, I think we have to sit on our hands. We have to resist the urge to 'fix'. The idea that we need to look good in order to be a good coach inhibits us and we need to be aware of that.

These days we live in a paradigm of finding answers. That's our world and we have to live in it until we get to a place of being able to say "I can't fix this and that is okay."

Let's look at an example of someone who works in an organisation where there's a paradigm of fixing things and imagine they've been promoted. Everyone expects them to feel excited and positive, and perhaps they do. They may also feel fear and anxiety. They might worry about being disliked. They were a colleague and now they are a line manager. They may have mixed feelings about that. If there's only space in the work culture for expressing positive feelings, then the other feelings can't be heard. If I'm only there for the positive as a coach, then the 'negative' feelings won't be heard in coaching either except as something to be fixed: "Here's your fear. How can I help you overcome it?" If I don't try to fix it then perhaps for the first time they may feel listened to for all that they are. It's an unfoldment, it moves away from taking them anywhere and towards what wants to manifest.

I believe passionately that the soul wants to be heard.

So often we get information and instructions about how to fix things: "I went on a great course and it might really help you.", "There's this really great book that you should read.", "Try speed-dating!" etc. One thing we've done in our increasingly rationalistic society is to create a solution for almost every problem or concern. But when we don't jump in with an immediate offer of a solution then something else is possible. The essence within a person starts to sing its own song. How often do we really get listened to?

There's a quotation from Pablo Neruda that I really love, and which speaks to the essence of what I do...

"I want to do for you what the spring does for the cherry trees."

If we as coaches can really listen then we can create the space for someone to blossom, just as the spring creates the space for the cherry tree to be the cherry tree in blossom. That's what I think masterful coaching is, simply allowing the space for what wants to manifest to manifest.

That kind of listening, from a place of being available, allows possibility. Imagine teachers able to create the space for what wants to be in precious young lives. Education is so often merely about giving information, such as learning the name of the Capital of Ethiopia or learning to produce something that can be assessed from the outside. That doesn't give a lot of space to what is there in the child, and this process continues into adult life as we endlessly produce more and more information, rather than living in exploration, curiosity, and, dare I say, uncertainty! I am reminded of a distinction between an 'expert' and a 'master'. The expert wants to get to the answer as quickly as possible. The master wants to stay in ignorance as long as possible and to stay in the exploration.

This can apply to all kinds of relationships whether they're personal, professional or political. For example, imagine how different a conversation between a husband and wife might be with more space given to just hanging out rather than saying we have to stay in this box together, or that you have to stay in that box. If I want to persuade you to take on my perspective, then there's only one measure of 'success' – that I have persuaded you of. If, however, I am open to us exploring together, then we expand the range of possibilities, and can create something together, which might be very different from my original box.

I remember the British politicians Tony Benn and David Davies setting up a series of conversations to explore issues together. Introducing the conversations, Tony Benn said that he didn't want to try and persuade David Davies of anything – he wanted them to have a context of exploring together, to see what two people of very different views could create in a mood of openness and curiosity.

Similarly, in business, if I'm in a meeting and I'm defensive or trying to put my argument across I'm not available. I'm just in a small box, trying to defend my perspective, so the conversation has very limited possibility - either I persuade you (I 'win'), or I don't (I 'lose'). However, if as in the example of Benn and Davies, I approach it from the perspective of seeing what we can create together, then something totally new becomes possible, and together we might create something of real value and inspiration.

I guess we can approach life from that spirit of curiosity – even at the supermarket checkout we may have a different kind of interaction if we maintain an openness, rather than merely being focused on getting our purchases out of the store as quickly as possible.

It is a different quality of presence, not just concerned with results but with what wants to manifest at this point in time. If I have a conversation which focuses on results only, when results are more important than relating to the person in front of me, then an opportunity is missed.

Asking, "What wants to manifest?" is a practice, just as meditation is a practice. It is about a way of being rather than a way of doing things. One keeps on trying to make the space for what wants to manifest. For example, rather than quickly jumping to the conclusion that a politician is being an idiot, you can ask the question, "What wants to manifest in what they are saying or doing?"

This is most definitely not just a coaching *technique*. It is about being curious, open, gentle, light and irreverent. By irreverent I mean I create lightness. I don't take myself too seriously and that can create the space for someone seeing with lightness what they might have been seeing with heaviness. It's like a child asking their father, "!Why Daddy? Why?" It might be annoying for the father being asked so many questions but the child is coming from a place of innocence. They just want to know why. I encourage people to explore their own questions with that innocent lightness, not from having to get anything right, and not from a place of forcing themselves to explore something that isn't comfortable.

How can you explore this question yourself? What happens if you allow yourself to honour your 'irrational' responses rather than judging them? Can you 'listen' to different parts of yourself other than your thinking mind when you are figuring out what to do, or how to 'make sense of' an experience? Where do you find yourself pulled away from your biological instincts? Take time to explore whether this really serves you, or whether it just fits into a 'rational' framework. Treat these explorations with lightness, not from having to get anything right, and not from a place of forcing yourself to explore things that are not comfortable.

When I work with coaches I want to move them to a place where they can hold the space of asking "What wants to manifest?"

Sir John Whitmore has said that the most important work for coaches was not more coaching training but continuing personal development work. Someone who never has to struggle wouldn't be a very good coach. In fact being messed up, and being aware of one's humanity and flaws, is a gift in being a coach. We coaches can sometimes fall into the trap of believing that we have to be 'sorted out', or have all the answers, before we can coach. But then we're back in the territory of being the expert, and are almost 'too clever' to coach – Rumi wrote:

"Sell your cleverness and buy bewilderedness" bewilderment, like the Buddhist concept of 'beginner's mind' is a great place from which to coach – then we can be open, curious, and willing to see what's there...

We, like our clients, are very much 'work in progress'. Again, Sir John Whitmore, speaking at the Association for Coaching conference in London, was talking about one of the functions of coaching being to help people explore the question "Who are you?" When asked by one of the audience who *he* was, he answered: "I'm still looking."

About the Author

Aboodi Shabi is one of the UK's most senior and well-known personal coaches. A pioneer and leader in the UK coaching community and former founding-President of UK International Coach Federation, Aboodi has also served the profession at all levels internationally.

He is an ICF Professional Certified Coach and is also certified with Newfield Network, for whom he is currently European Programme Manager and a member of their mentor coaching team. He is also an external assessor for the Academy of Executive Coaching. A sought-after mentor coach and speaker specialising in coach mastery and coaching to the soul, he has worked with hundreds of coaches across Europe and in North America, individually, in presentations and in workshops.

Learn more about Aboodi and his work here: www.aboodi.net

Judy Barber

WHAT IS YOUR QUESTION?

BY LOURDES CALLEN

As we become aware of ourselves and discover the world in the first years of life we naturally ask questions. To find our way in life we can look in two different directions, towards the world outside and towards the world inside. As the inner world awakens so do thoughtful questions. When I was nine I had the first deeper question that I remember: "Why are adults like that?" In my forties I am still asking this, a quest for understanding human nature. Our questions reflect our individuality. Finding 'our questions' will help us find our way.

Questions Contain Solutions.

In organisations and relationships, good questions and willingness to change are part of progress. Questions can contain solutions and can lead to the next steps. When we meet questions as blessings rather than with dread they can bring the new breath of what wants to be. It is a sign of the times that something is brewing in people's spirits. It moves us to ask questions about the world and to improve situations we find ourselves in.

By daring to really look inside ourselves we can perceive questions to take our relationships and fragile world forward. Then we can perceive our outer and inner realities more clearly and objectively, without adding negativity or superficial positivity.

- Encourage people to look inside to find questions that lead to constructive change.

Questions About The Present Times.

In some ways human beings seem to be growing apart from each other. Making sure we keep and build our material possessions can seem more important than other people.

233

After listening to the world news recently a friend said, "I want to find a space to think about what is happening." People seem to have an impulse to digest the news through talking, writing, meditating or asking, "What can I do to change this state of affairs?" Strong questions are coming up for all humanity.

Recent disasters seem to have an awakening effect, connecting us with what is most human in us. We want to give and receive and to build bridges. Disasters get us talking to each other, making us share vulnerability as well as strength. We grow together as we face big events. They are wake-up calls to awareness of our humanity and of the earth.

We see the global picture and ask: "What is the world situation asking from me?" Perhaps we feel small, or unable to reach so far. Can a change in me influence the global situation? What if by changing ourselves we are changing the world to a greater degree than we can possibly imagine? It appears more and more that individual people can contribute to the world by working with self transformation.

- Encourage people to notice the effect of inner transformation in the world around them.

How can I change?

We may be functioning with familiar old ingrained automatic habits that can be unhelpful. Something has to come in place of holding on to structures that no longer work. However, the new is unknown, and even if it is better, part of us may still resist it. A question that can help you to break old habits is: "What can I do today that is different?" Actions in response to that question might seem insignificant at the outset but they build over time. Examples of this might be:

- Going to sleep earlier to get enough rest
- Switching off the TV
- Stopping a habitual reaction to someone close to us
- Curbing negativity about an aspect of life
- Resisting feeling like a victim in a particular relationship

Small changes can lead to being more of who we really are and to greater accomplishment. Through making such changes we can mature in our inner life, and achieve detachment from outdated behaviour and a stronger connection with the world.

- Encourage people to experiment with breaking habits, at first in small ways.

Trusting The Inner World.

Women and men are longing for change. Children are craving for change, yet we live in a culture of entertainment that leads to passivity. The world could definitely benefit from change. It is time for questions that will have an awakening effect on us.

When we find a quick fix or answer we can feel better instantly because we have got a system or a recipe that we can apply, but we aren't necessarily more awake. Each situation is different and a solution from outside might not actually fit. However when we observe and listen to what is happening inside as well as around us we can trust ourselves more and develop the courage to take action.

Will others solve my problems from the outside or does change happen within me? The latter requires will power and dynamic thinking.

This is a new way of approaching questions and solutions that makes room for the future to talk to us. It keeps us open to exploring. Inspiration and intuition can be present and we can find the best possible step for each life situation.

"How can we make relationships and communication work?" "How do we bring the experience of childhood back to children?" There is not always a straightforward answer to the questions of our time but we need to ponder on them to deepen our lives. As we gain confidence in listening to our questions, we might notice how life itself responds to them.

- Rather than giving people answers or quick fixes, encourage them to be more active in noticing what they are thinking and feeling. That helps them to trust and strengthen themselves.

Finding Our Questions

The path of finding and working with questions is one through which we change. What questions live in us? When we notice our questions we become inwardly active. They may be individual or shared. We can ask, "What do I need to develop in myself?" In a group once someone asked "How do we bring our ideals into practical reality?" People found this interesting because the question was common to them all. It brought them alive and in touch with themselves. We felt more animated.

How do we discriminate between all the different questions we may have and the *one* which is essential? When asked: "What is your question?" we might find questions that are not yet the main one. We may be exploring different aspects of a given problem and with exploration as a background look for the question that emerges.

Clarity comes when we can formulate the question that speaks to us most and reflects our main concern – the one that defines best where I am now. It could be "How can I make this work?", "What can I do to strengthen myself?" or "What will give our children a secure foundation in life?" Once we find a question form that contains the main essence it focuses us, clarifies where we are now and opens the way forward.

- By listening carefully you may be able to detect someone's question and ask: "Is this your question?"

Which Question Is Most Important at A Particular Time?

The essential one makes me feel in touch with myself and activates my inner self. If I ask: "Is there a gap between what I am saying and what I am doing?" I am on the road towards uniting inner intentions with outer reality. I might notice the question changing over time and awakening subtly different feelings, or I might notice new questions. That is an example of the art of discovering an emerging question, expressing it and noticing how it changes.

Questions open the way to meeting the future and bringing it about. It takes time for them to be perceived in our inner world, expressed and then carried with us. Sometimes we have to live with a question that is part of 'the riddle of life' and it only gets solved over time.

Living with questions brings home the need for inner strengthening. Then we can feel all right even though we do not have all the answers or solutions yet.

- You can help someone to discover their current question, to reformulate it and to refine it.
- You can encourage people to live with questions that may change, to leave them open, and to perceive new questions.
- You might also need to help people find the inner strength for living with as-yet unanswered questions, and for feeling content in the meantime.

Working With Groups

In groups it is important that people feel they can ask questions. People's questions are enriching because they show their concerns, interests or impulses. Questions may be seen as challenges to established patterns, but can actually be a sign of the will to pick up positive new impulses coming from the future.

New forms for living in today's world can make themselves visible when people work with questions. In a group conversation after a talk someone said: "This is the third talk where I have come intending to solve my problems and answer my questions. Now I realize that what I am doing is opening up and generating new questions." Her learning process was activated by questions. It led to her making discoveries about how she wanted to relate to her son and to find valuable insights. The process of asking questions was more important than finding instant answers.

People learn and move forward when they concentrate on what is real for them. Questions are close to their hearts and that motivates them! As a facilitator, coach or colleague you can introduce your ideas but it works better to connect your ideas with their questions. It enables them to be more engaged.

- When running a group make sure people feel they can risk asking questions and make time to discuss people's questions.
- Motivate people by working with their questions.
- You can bring your input to people, but connect it to *their* questions.

Unnecessary Questions

When someone is presented with too many questions they cannot easily take them in. Challenging questions may be met with resistance. When building a picture of another person's situation, asking too many questions is not always justified. When we ask unnecessary questions and receive a dense fabric of information in response it can take away our focus from what is important. Questions asked out of curiosity are felt as invasions and they close doors. They tend not to gather important details and irritate the person who is being 'interrogated'. When questions come from genuine interest, compassion or love doors can open and someone is encouraged to ponder further. Asking questions is an art that needs developing. Listening is of course just as important. How could questions ever be expressed if nobody received them?

- Don't ask too many questions or ask questions for information you don't really need.
- Just ask genuine questions from love and compassion.
- Learn the art of when to ask questions – and of when to listen!

Learning And Growing Through Life Experiences

Questions lead to other questions through a path of learning as we journey through life. Are we ready to ask the question or are we prepared to miss this chance? Life seems to keep bringing another opportunity until we are back on track and learning can be found even from things on our path which we don't especially like. The journey reveals who we are and what we are here to do. In biography work people can learn from their past in a way that can inspire them in how they live from now on.

In my biography work I met a young woman who was very happy studying Art Therapy. She told me how a few years before she had been studying economics in Barcelona and lived near La Sagradia Familia, a famous cathedral by the architect Gaudi. She passed it every day and kept noticing new things about it. I listened carefully and asked her how that experience influenced her decision to move away from economics to study Art Therapy. She had not thought of that. However, later she realised that Gaudi's influence had opened a new sensitivity to art in her.

Questions like that can reveal meanings, stimulate inner activity and awaken the self. When we observe and listen to our biographies we may find previously hidden inner wisdom.

Another time this woman considered what might really have motivated her to live there.

"Life brought that possibility to me when I was in search of my next step." She lived with the question and life brought the answer. She spent a long time wondering what to do after studying economics and in fact the answer was not very far away.

- Encourage people to find learnings even from things they didn't like at the time.
- Encourage people to find inspiration by understanding their past.
- Ask people questions that may reveal the meaning of their path.

La Sagradia Familia - Barcelona

What Is Your Question?

So, can you find your question, and your answer, from within yourself? What habits can you break in order to allow change? What in your life is already introducing your future to you? Can you find clues in your past? Can you find the strength to live with your question while it develops and perhaps changes? How will you work with questions in groups? And how will *you* contribute to the world through developing your inner life?

We can explore and discover the emerging questions contained in each situation and phase of life. Sometimes by letting questions go and looking back at them again over time we can discern which are still relevant.

In my experience life brings new opportunities and openings as a result of inner activity with questions. It is a journey in which new answers and possibilities for the future make themselves clear.

About the Author

I walk my path with plenty of questions about life and how to live it. I am still looking for ways of observing and learning from life and find this fascinating.

Questions about my own task in life brought me to England where I trained in Steiner Early Education. The inspiring depth of understanding of the human being that I found impregnated my future work. After a few years teaching, my interest in social arts and adult learning led to Social and Personal Development training.

Since then I have activated life-sharing groups in which we hear the emerging questions of our time, how our world is changing and what we may contribute. I enjoy creating spaces where qualities of interest in each other and listening can be alive again. My Biographical and Counselling studies and practice have added understanding of the soul and our human destiny.

The two important threads running through my life are concern about children's well-being and about adult growth and social awareness. These find expression in the 'A Time for Childhood' initiative. This includes working on parenting questions in groups, individual conversations and writing projects. Courses on the 'Art of Living' run alongside. These include biography workshops, in which we look at our lives in a way that gives new perspective. This work has been offered for ten years in England and Spain. The article 'A New Awareness for Childhood' was published by New View in London 2003. I am writing a book, 'A Time for Childhood', on the importance of a time for childhood in the journey of life. I run courses in schools and organisations and I offer individual consultations which create space for working with personal questions.

Find out more about Lourdes Callen: www.atimeforchildhood.com

Judy Barber

WHAT QUESTIONS CAN YOU ASK?

BY JUDY BARBER

This chapter draws the book to a close as I ask you to look at the process of asking questions in coaching conversations and in other situations. The different writers have all shown you questions they use, many of which are their own creations, and all of which are someone's creation. Here is an invitation to find and create your own questions, and to use them in your own unique way. So I ask you now to think...

"What questions can you ask?"

As a coaching question "What questions can you ask?" is useful in a similar way to questions like:

"If you were coaching someone who was in a situation like this how would you coach them?"

It invites you to utilise your own resources. It intimates that one doesn't have to accept things as they appear but that you can find out more. I would also ask, "What questions can you ask?" of someone who was dealing with a complex situation, perhaps attempting to make a decision while in a state of shock or overwhelm. Someone might not have considered checking out the facts behind an assumption they are making or behind what they are being told is true. Finding out more might help them out of feeling stuck or to dismantle a bias.

"What questions do you need to ask?"

"Who could tell you more about that?"

"How could you test that assumption?"

"Is there anything else you need to know"

How Can I Make Up New Questions?

I know that my best questions arise naturally in conversation. I may have used them before, borrowed them from other people or they may be new, but in a sense they are all new when they arrive fresh in the conversation, made available thoughtfully at a good moment. I know when I do this well because I sense shifts in the other person or the group, but what is the mechanism of creating the question? How can I learn to do it better? How can I enable others to make up new questions?

There I go, asking questions again. As I think about the questions I have just asked answers are beginning to flood in like e-mails on a Monday morning. Which thought do I open first? Which thought will I forget if I don't deal with it right now? Which thought just has to have a response immediately? Which thoughts are the mind-equivalent of spam – boring repetitive mind chatter – that need to be deleted? Which thought do I want to open because it looks interesting? Which thought am I drawn to because I sense it is important in some way? The first answer that came up was that the secret is asking the questions, simply that, asking the questions and seeing what follows.

A different image that comes up is of prayer, asking the question of a 'higher being' and waiting for the answer to arrive, when and in whatever form.

With a client I might hold onto a question I would like to ask and then find they are answering it anyway in their own way. I often take a question I am working with for myself into sleep and find that the answer, or at least a shift in approach, comes into my thoughts as I wake up. The question has usually lost some of the emotional charge I had loaded onto it and the answer is better than I could have found the day before. There are implications in that for coaching, especially if either the coach, the client or both are after a quick solution.

Finding an answer may be premature and sometimes the best action for a client to take after a session may be to go away and reflect further on a question for a while. That's the wisdom of saying "I'll sleep on that."

What I experience in coaching is that questions 'arrive'. That might sound a bit odd. Of course I'm very conscious of putting precise words together so I don't mean they just appear fully formed in my mind. As

I experience it, I have my attention fully in the listening. When doing telephone coaching all my attention is with the voice of the person on the phone. I might take rough notes, for example of what someone wants and what they are feeling, and I'm remembering what's already been said as well as listening to what is being said now. It's similar with face to face coaching except that then I'm watching expressions and movement as well and don't manage many notes at the time.

So, after some listening there might come a moment when I sense what they are *now* saying they want isn't congruent with what they *were* saying earlier. For example, someone might be saying they want to start some freelance work in the evening as well as doing their day job, as a way towards starting a new business. I might gently ask: "How will that fit with your wish for less stress and more time with your partner?" The question links two aspects of their life so that they can weigh up different needs. This might lead them towards finding a different way to take steps towards their business idea. It's a simple example of a helpful coaching question born of listening. It 'arrived' out of careful listening and perhaps taking notes.

The experience of having questions, and images too, 'arrive' is often called intuition. That can be a confusing word because people tend to define it differently and I suspect that we all have differing experiences that we call intuition. It's an interesting subject for philosophical, psychological, and spiritual research. Here I just want to point to the fact that, for me at least, although the experience is that the question 'arrives', it's been preceded by attentive listening and making connections between different parts of what someone is expressing. When people say something like "That's very intuitive!", for me it has usually been a very conscious, and obvious, process based on careful listening. I say this because it points to intuition being something that can be developed in life, and with experience of coaching and other forms of helpful conversations, rather than as something one just has, as if by magic or chance.

What Questions Can I Ask Myself?

I have questions which I don't voice:

"Should I share an idea of mine here?"

"How can I respond in a way that won't overload this person?"

"How can I make a suggestion in a way that lets her feel free to take it, or not?"

"Of all the things I feel like blurting out, what, if anything, would it be helpful for me to say right now?"

"Is it better to keep quiet now?'"

"What's going on now that their tone of voice has changed?"

"What encouragement can I give?"

When I ask myself questions like these as a coach and find the answers inside me, I am consciously working towards creating a good speaking space for someone. Aboodi Shabi's question, "What wants to manifest?" is a question like that.

Another question someone might need to ask is whether they are wanting or tending to ask too many questions. That might be from curiosity. Curiosity is definitely appreciated when it allows someone feel listened to or to gain clarity, but at other times curiosity might be something to keep in check.

Asking yourself questions to filter what you feel like saying before speaking out can help to avoid speaking from habit and can also help you to be very conscious of speaking in a way that supports the other in that moment. It's that kind of attention to detail that marks out a coaching conversation.

Breaking Habits And Maintaining Vitality

If you identify habits that need rooting out, making up some questions might help. Examples might be:

"How much am I speaking in this conversation?"

"Am I keeping what they are telling me separate in my mind from what has happened in my own life?"

"Should I listen a bit longer first?"

"Is it my place to fix this?"

Personally, I like to be on my toes with new questions for myself so that I stay alert, flexible and responsive to the person I'm conversing with.

What Questions Do I Need To Ask?

Having said that asking inner questions is important, questioning yourself every time you want to open your mouth might be too limiting! If you are too self-critical or blocked by limited self-esteem you might stop yourself too much. Out of fear of getting it 'wrong' you might not ask the question that could create a wonderful possibility. When I'm not sure about the relevance of a question but have a strong sense that it would be good to ask it I come out with things like: "I'm not sure if this fits, but have you considered...?" That gives the client space to accept or reject.

Obviously there's some kind of balance to be struck here; being humble enough to acknowledge where improvement is needed and accepting that you are already doing your best in a good-hearted way. Perhaps if someone just generally senses that you are taking care with how you conduct a conversation then that allows them to be their whole self and that is good enough for now. Over time awareness can be sharpened and skill with questioning developed.

How Can I Get Better At Asking Questions?

The first answer to that question is listening. Listening just has to be the starting point for any coaching. Listening, listening and more listening. On this subject I'd like to recommend Nancy Cline's book 'Time to Listen'. Listening is the stage-set for questions. There are a lot of questions together in this book because it is a reference book, but no one is suggesting getting frenetic about asking questions!

There's a lot more listening in a coaching conversation than there is questioning.

I also think it is important to be relaxed and clear-headed and not to be attached to a particular outcome. It helps if you are not frightened of opening up topics that might be culturally or personally uncomfortable. Other background qualities to develop are: not hurrying, being optimistic and friendly but also staying detached while maintaining empathy.

Other important background factors are moods and attitudes. If you push for a particular result or solution, or if you have a strong opinion about what is right or what should happen it adds a particular dynamic to the conversation that can have dangerous consequences.

If, however, you are more personally detached from the outcome and more relaxed than the other person then they can focus on their own motivation and you can put your energy into being receptive to their agenda. That way the truly good question has more chance of emerging if it is needed.

How Can I Use Coaching Questions In Conversations And Meetings?

The situation is somewhat different from coaching when I'm having an ordinary conversation or taking part in a meeting. For example, I may quite legitimately want something specific to happen or want to express a particular opinion. However, unless my only point of interest is dominating the situation, it still serves me to stay open to what other people bring and to create space for that. Coaching questions are invaluable in many kinds of conversation because they encourage people.

By asking questions I can enable the conversation to open up in a positive way. In my mind I could be asking questions such as:

"What question could I ask to create common ground here?"

"What question could I ask to bring out what's not being said?"

"What could I say to bring some love or warmth into this?"

Out loud I might ask questions such as:

"What else do we need to be considering?"

"Who else is this going to effect?"

"Why are we seeing this so very differently from each other when we have similar visions?"

"If we can't reach an agreement now, how might we work towards an agreement in the future?"

Can I Put That As A Question?

Often just forming things you want to say into questions is more gentle than making statements. Importantly this could be turning a negative thought such as: "No way! That's never going to work." into a question:

"How would that work?"

Just that simple device in a fast-moving conversation can prevent two people becoming polarised over an issue and antagonistic towards each other. The question form invites further communication. I'm not suggesting that one never makes a clear statement of opinion, but I am inviting you to consider working with questions to leave things open. I'm suggesting this might be really helpful at emotionally charged moments. Questions can create reflective space between people and defuse tensions. They can move a conversation towards understanding and allow people to create positive outcomes even when a positive outcome had seemed unlikely. There are very interesting implications here for all kinds of politics!

In coaching conversations I use questions as a graceful way of offering my thoughts and perceptions, and of enabling the conversation to move along. I might say things like:

"Can I share some ideas here?"

"Would you like me to tell you an anecdote about a similar situation?"

"Would you like me to suggest a book that discusses that topic?"

"Can I recap some of the different parts of what you have been telling me?"

The question form allows the client or other speaking partner to stay in control and to consider how they want you to work with them. Many conversations, in professional and other contexts, mix coaching and mentoring and questions such as those can keep the distinction between the two clear: the client can say no.

Questions are also great in ordinary conversations between friends when similar experiences are being shared. Just changing, "It was like that with my last boyfriend." To, "I wonder if you are feeling anything like I was when Herbert dumped me?" allows each person's experiences to be distinct. Empathy, rather than bundling different experiences together in a confusing or negative way, becomes possible.

In this chapter I've gathered together various suggestions, possibilities and thoughts about asking questions, and they lead to this most important question:

What Questions Will Work For You?

That's one I can't answer, but I'd love to know the answers! In fact I'll put that as a question!

"Please would you write and tell me what happens as a result of reading this book?"

I am looking forward to the answers I get to that one!

A CALL TO ACTION

Here is a koan, one of those puzzling questions favoured in Japanese Zen Buddhism for creating a change of state, except that this one is a stack of three questions and is traditional Jewish:

> "If I am not for me, then who is for me?
> If I am just for me, then who am I?
> And if not now, then when?"

Good Question! has given you opportunities to investigate the thoughts, questions and activities of twenty eight people who are all busy making differences to the quality of life. Of course the contributors are expert in their fields, but I doubt any would want to be set apart as better able to create change than you, the reader, whatever your current circumstances.

And so I want to tell a little science fiction story that I remember from years ago in the infancy of the computer. Scientists from around the world – and isn't it nice that they decided to work together on this! – gathered all the resources, knowledge and inventiveness of the different societies together to build the ultimate computer. On the appointed day, with all the world dignitaries, media reporters and religious leaders present there was a special opening ceremony in which the ultimate question was to be asked. People around the world were glued to TV sets and radios. The Secretary General of the United Nations stepped forward to cut the red tape and pose the ultimate question, which was: "Is there a God?". The breath of the world was baited as the valves flickered and the tapes whirred. And then the answer came, tapped out letter by letter on the little grey screen. "NOW there is!

And why am I telling you this? It's because it's a joke about all those individual people around the world handing over their power to the mechanical authority of the computer, when the answer to the question was one for them each to discover in their own way. I want this book to contribute to a new kind of joining of individual human hearts and minds, each with resources, knowledge and inventiveness to share for the purpose of bringing about positive change in many different fields.

I often hear people saying *'Good Question!'* in conversation and so I think people have a natural readiness to welcome and respond to questions. We are glad when someone asks a good question because it makes something new possible in the conversation. People will appreciate you asking them good questions.

I wonder what you make of the questions we have posed and how you are thinking of using them. Unlike the people in that story, I hope you'll be making the questions your own and finding good answers that go beyond formulas in real situations.

I doubt the author of that story could have foreseen the value of computers for people communicating around the world, but that is how it is now. We've provided our website details so you can find out more about us and our activities. We hope you get in touch.

There's plenty for us all to do to make the world a better place and we wish you joy in asking good questions as you go about your lives and work.

And if you doubt that you can make much difference, take heart from the American anthropologist Margaret Mead:

"Never doubt that a small group of thoughtful, committed citizens can change the world. Indeed, it is the only thing that ever has."

...and then think of how many people are busy in their circles of influence and of yourself in your circles of influence.

ABOUT JUDY BARBER

When she landed at Dover off an ocean liner, Judy could still hear the sounds of her Zulu Nanny singing. She was a Surrey grammar school girl doing sciences, with a taste for drama fed by Christmas parties with cockney music hall relatives. She danced through student life in Brighton reading novels, dressing in 1940s frocks and learning from enlightened lecturers how to teach teenagers and adults.

She has taught English, literature, drama and more in prison, technical college, Iran, Rudolf Steiner School and in the community to every age. She has cooked French food in Paris, collected Balinese paintings, sat with Buddhist teachers in Devon and Thailand, edited and written for magazines, run workshops, acted, helped found a school in New Zealand, owned and run a B&B and done up old houses. She's studied art therapy and anthroposophy, and been on inspiring seminars with the best. She enjoys many things and in a parallel universe she might be a basket maker, an interior designer, an inventor, a spiritual friend of sorts, a playwright or a director.

She has a B.Ed in English, psychology and education, and certificates in Drama Therapy, NLP Practitioner level, Newcastle College Performance Coaching and Fraser Clarke Business Coaching. She's an International Coach Federation member and a Social Artist.

Judy believes we can 'have it all' by finding balance, bringing our own dreams into reality and giving to life. People choose to work with Judy to achieve personal, career and business goals and when they want their lives to matter. People she meets need to be contributing and feel painful frustration until they are. Her vision is for things to work out in the 21st century, and so her book is about evolving communication. Life is changing and people need inspiration, and to experience their lives as necessary parts of the big picture.

Judy loves interesting conversations and relates to the whole gamut of relationships and group dynamics, so she works one to one and with groups, inviting people to develop confidence and creativity, and finding questions encouraging clarity, fresh thought and moving forward. People can allow different aspects of themselves to blossom. Her clients come from a wide personal and geographical background, including business people, coaches, writers, and those using coaching and facilitation skills; a diverse group sharing a common desire to make unique contributions to life.

Her work is writing, including for Resource Magazine www.resourcemagazine.com, coaching, creating seminars for personal and business development and freelance facilitation.

Learn more about Judy and her work at www.judybarber.net

Lightning Source UK Ltd.
Milton Keynes UK
14 May 2010

154206UK00001B/25/A